level 1

UNLOCKING THE SECRETS OF PLAYING

drums

Noam Lederman
Series Creator and Supervisory Editor

James Pethoridge

Published by **Winner** Music Pte Ltd
707 East Coast Road
Singapore 459063
Singapore

ISBN 978–1–910762–00–4
VV00001
© VVinner Music 2016

Series creator and supervisory editor: Noam Lederman
Written by Noam Lederman
Music engraving: Tom Fleming
Edited by Tom Fleming
Photography: Matthew Ward
Additional photography: Chiko Photography
Personality images courtesy of Corbis
Cover and book design: Chloë Alexander Design
Special thanks to Theron Lim and Jai Dzafir

www.vvinner.com
www.noamlederman.com

Contents

▶⤸ Free Downloads

- *Graded pieces: demonstration & backing tracks*

- *Ear training exercises*

Visit **vvinner.com/downloads**

Introduction

Welcome to *Unlocking the Secrets of Playing Drums Level 1*.

This book is for every drum and beat enthusiast around the globe. It was designed to reveal the secrets of becoming a successful drummer. The book will encourage you to develop using the most efficient learning method according to your technique. Although the book is self-explanatory and you will be able to go through it on your own, a good teacher will help make the process quicker and ensure that you do not develop any unwanted habits in the early stages.

Unlocking the Secrets of Playing Drums Level 1 has five sections: Foundation, Debut, Grade 1, Grade 2 and Grade 3. It includes detailed explanations of the techniques required to master any music exam. However, if your main purpose in using this book is in preparation for a performance exam it is essential to check the specific criteria of the grade that you intend to take.

Throughout the book, you will be encouraged to develop your creativity and individuality as well as enhance both your aural and reading skills in order to become the best musician you can be.

Remember that everyone learns in a different way and you will need to identify the most efficient learning method for you as an individual. This is the key to unlocking the secrets of playing drums.

I hope that you find this book useful and enjoy the journey of becoming a successful drummer.

Noam Lederman, series creator

The Drum Kit

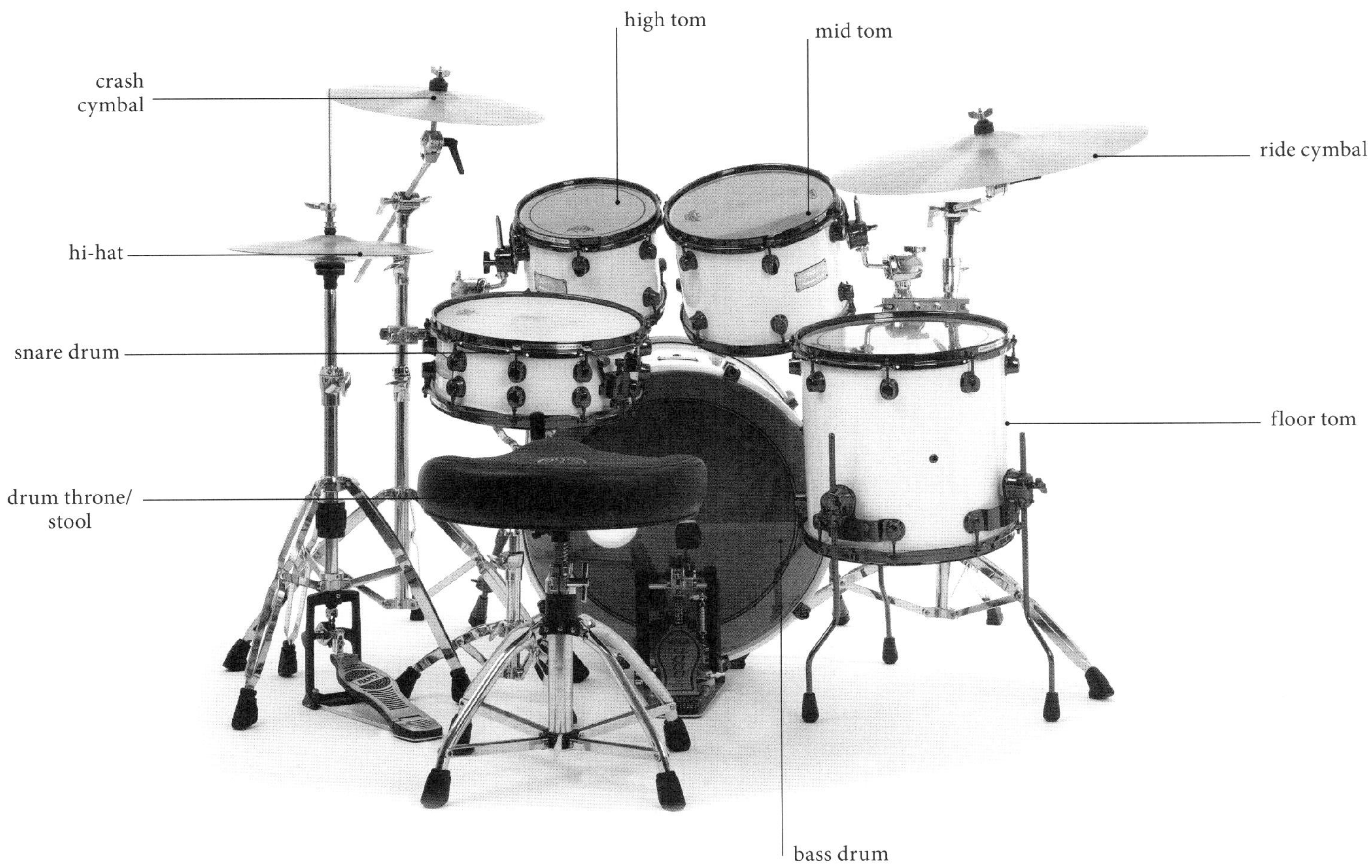

crash cymbal

high tom

mid tom

ride cymbal

hi-hat

snare drum

drum throne/ stool

floor tom

bass drum

Acoustic or Electronic?

Unlocking the Secrets of Playing Drums is designed for the acoustic drum kit, therefore the techniques described, sound production and dynamic control are all related to the acoustic drum kit. However, many beginners choose to play an electronic drum kit. There are many clear advantages to this: it takes much less space than the acoustic kit, it can be played with headphones to minimise the noise level, and it is easier to achieve a balanced sound. If you decide to use an electronic kit you can still follow this series and develop as a drummer. However, it is recommended that whenever possible you play an acoustic kit as well in order to transfer the techniques discussed and develop the sensitivity required to play acoustic drums well.

Many modern drummers choose to add electronic drums to their acoustic setups in order to achieve certain sounds. A drum kit with both acoustic and electronic components is known as a hybrid kit.

The Drum Stick

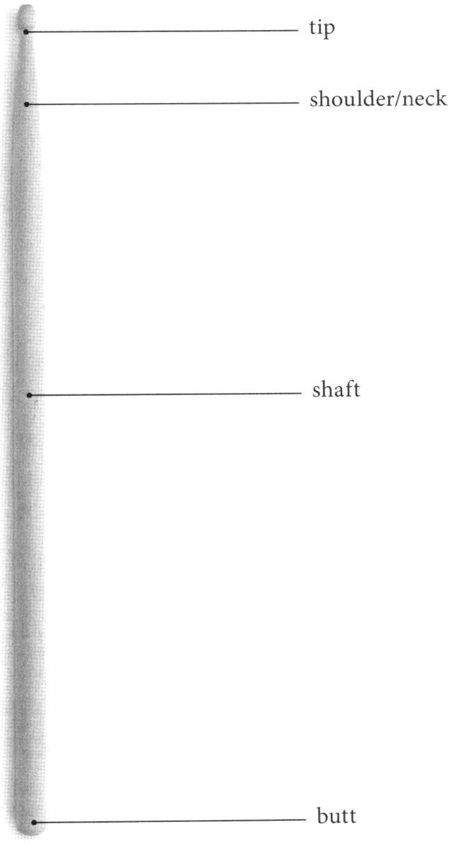

tip

shoulder/neck

shaft

butt

Setting Up Your Drum Kit

Bass Drum

Place the bass drum where required, ensuring that the legs are secured and the drum is level and balanced.

Bass Drum Pedal

Although every bass drum pedal is slightly different, there will always be a way to attach the pedal to the rim of the bass drum. Ensure that the pedal is level and completely flat on the floor, then secure and tighten the pedal onto the rim.

Snare Drum

Place the snare on the drum stand. Most stands have a three-pronged claw that grips the drum. Ensure that this is tightened to hold the drum securely. Choose the height that suits your body and the angle of the snare that feels most comfortable. You may need to adjust this a few times until you find the best position for you. Place the snare drum stand with the snare in front and slightly to the left of the bass drum. (This applies to right-handed drummers. Left-handed players should set the kit up the other way around and reverse all references in this book from right to left.)

Some left-handed players choose to play open-handed where the left hand plays on the hi-hat and the right hand on the snare without crossing the hands. To play open-handed, reverse all references in this book from left to right or follow the left-handed sticking.

Hi-Hat

After setting the bottom and top hi-hat cymbals on the hi-hat stand, place it next to the snare drum. Remember that the hi-hat clutch is supposed to hold the top hi-hat cymbal but not to choke it, so do not over-tighten the clutch when setting it up. Ensure that the hi-hat and bass drum pedals are in the most comfortable position for your body. This usually means that the hi-hat pedal will be angled inwards slightly. Now, let's focus on your seating position. Sit on your drum throne facing forward and check if the angle of both pedals is comfortable for you. Make minor adjustments to both pedals until you achieve the optimum seating position. Try to memorise your position in relation to the pedals and snare so you can easily achieve this in the future on any drum kit.

Toms

The setup of the toms can vary
between brands of drum kit, but the
basic concept remains the same.
Set up the toms using the holders
provided with the drum kit and
secure them so they stay in position.
Ensure that the toms and floor tom
are tilted towards you slightly; this
should make hitting the middle
of the drum easier. The high and
mid toms should be set as close
as possible to each other without
touching.

This way it will be easier for you to
move from one tom to another.

Cymbals

Set up the cymbal stands. Place the
ride cymbal on one stand and the
crash cymbal on the other.
Position the ride cymbal to your
right and the crash cymbal to
your left. Experiment and find the
most comfortable position for the
cymbals within the drum kit.

Tip!

*In order to ensure that the components of the drum kit stay exactly in place, you might want to consider
using a drum mat. If you do not have a specific drum mat, any large carpet should do the job too.
In addition, you can mark the position of each stand on the mat so it will be
straightforward to set up if you are moving the drum kit.*

Tuning Your Drum Kit

Before we cover the basics of tuning it is essential to discuss another element: drumheads. It is important to experiment with different drumheads to find what works best for each musical situation you encounter.

Drumheads

There are many different types of drumheads available today. These include:

Single ply: The most commonly used drumheads in the world. These are made from a single sheet (ply) of Mylar and offer high-end ring and overtones. Single ply heads are sensitive but the least durable of all top heads. They are ideal for lighter playing, but can also produce a boomy sound in more ambient situations. Examples: Evans G1, Remo Ambassador and Aquarian Classic Clear.

Double ply: These heads offer a deeper and controlled sound with more defined attack and a shorter sustain. Double ply heads are favoured by heavy rock drummers because of their high durability and punchy sound. Examples: Evans G2, Aquarian Super-2 and Remo Emperor.

Coated: Coated drumheads have a warmer tone, producing a brighter, less controlled sound with more attack. These are frequently used on the toms by jazz drummers. Examples: Evans G1 Coated, Aquarian Texture Coated and Remo Coated Ambassador.

Pre-muffled: These heads with varying amounts of muffling are most often used on the bass drum.

Speciality heads: Most manufacturers have a whole line of unusual speciality heads. Experiment and see what you can achieve by using these drumheads.

Resonant: These heads are used on the bottom side of the drum and they vary in thickness. Thinner resonant heads have less sustain and brighter tone so choose the thickness that suits your style of playing.

Tuning

Every modern drum kit has drums with two drumheads: the bottom head (resonant head) and the top head (batter head). Both heads must be evenly tightened with a drum key. Many drummers use the 'star method' in which you tighten opposite sides of the head until you reach the optimum sound. However, you can also tune the drum clockwise or anti-clockwise as long as you do it in a balanced way. Remember that the snare drum has one unique feature compared with the other drums: the snare wires. When changing the bottom head of a snare drum you will need to remove the snare wires and secure them back in place after the head is tuned. There is also a snare strainer mechanism that allows you to adjust the tightness of the snare wires. You may want to experiment with this before deciding on your preferred snare sound.

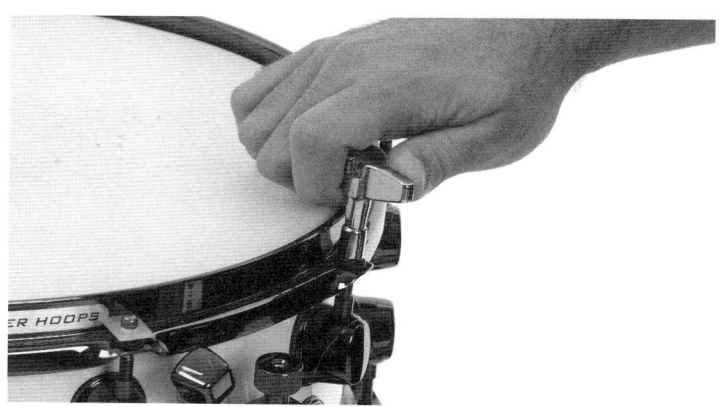

Toms

The process of tuning the tom is similar to tuning a snare drum. Start by ensuring that both heads are secured to the shell of the drum by the rim and supporting tension bolts. Then start tightening the bolts evenly and get rid of any wrinkles in the head. The next step is to create an even tone from each tom as well as a balanced sound from your toms overall. It is most common to tune the bottom head first and follow with the top head. We suggest tuning the bottom head slightly higher than the top head and adjust according to taste.

There are many factors that will help you decide which sound you want your toms to produce. These include the style of music, the size of the drums and your technique. For now it is important to get comfortable with the process and concept of tuning. More specific tuning advice will be given later in this series.

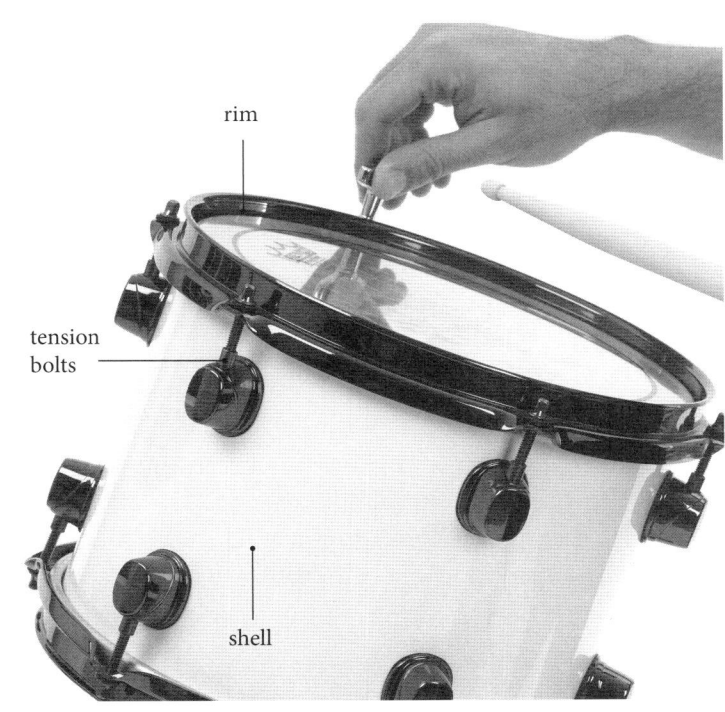

rim

tension bolts

shell

Bass Drum

Although it may take time to achieve the best sound from your bass drum, it will not require as much attention as the other drums in the kit on a regular basis. A bass drumhead will also last longer than any snare or tom head as it is struck by a soft beater, as opposed to the hard wooden tip of a drum stick. When tuning the bass drumheads, aim to keep them as loose as possible but still secured to the rim of the drum. Aim to avoid any wrinkles without over-tightening the drumhead. If the bass drum sound is not right for you, start tightening the heads gradually until you reach the desired sound.

A pillow or small duvet can be placed inside the bass drum and help achieve a punchy bass drum sound. Many drummers make a hole in the resonant bass drum head so they can use more or less damping depending on the style of music. This hole can also be used to insert a microphone.

Posture

It is crucial that you find a comfortable position when playing the drums, so spend time until you reach the optimum position for your body and technique. It is important to ensure that the body is relaxed, the back is straight and that you can easily reach every part of the drum kit.

Good posture – overhead view

Good posture – side view

The height of the drum throne is also very important for your posture. Set the throne so that your thighs are parallel to the floor – this will ensure that the whole foot is relaxed and can move in the most efficient and quick way.

In order to play the pedals in the most relaxed way, ensure that you do not sit too close to the drum kit. If you feel any strain when playing the pedals it is probably because you are sitting too close.

Sitting too far from the kit

Tip!

Keeping your shoulders relaxed will allow you to drum faster, move more easily and play for longer.

Bad posture – tense shoulders

Cymbal positioned too far away

Grip and Hand Technique

When gripping a drumstick use your index finger and thumb to secure the stick and curl the other three fingers to support the grip. Aim to hold the stick tight enough for it to be controlled well but not so tight that you feel any stress or discomfort.

There are two types of grip: matched grip and traditional grip. In matched grip both hands hold the stick in the same way. However, in traditional grip the hands hold the sticks in different ways. Matched grip is more popular today, but traditional grip is still used, mostly by drummers that specialise in jazz.

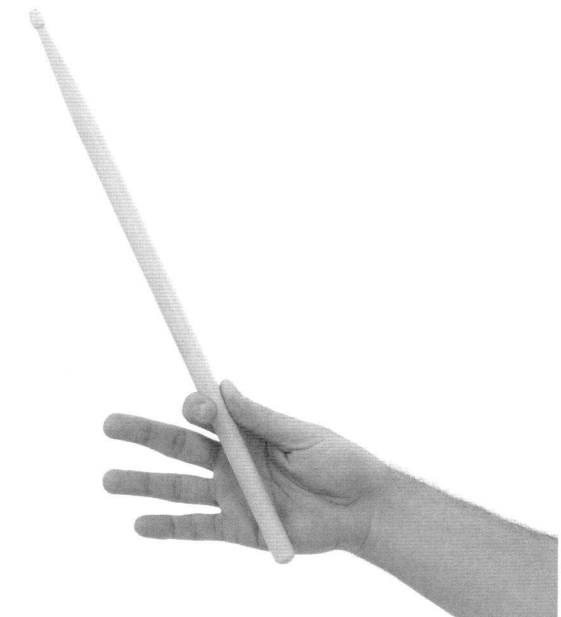

Step 1: Use the index finger and thumb to secure the stick

Matched Grip

Step 2: Curl the other three fingers to support the grip

Traditional Grip
To achieve this grip, let your first finger curl around the stick, then bring your second, third and fourth fingers gently around onto the stick to guide and stabilise it.

Stroke Types

There are four basic strokes that can be used when playing the drums:

- **Full stroke**
- **Down stroke**
- **Up stroke**
- **Tap Stroke**

The four strokes above can be achieved by using two main hand positions: high and low. In the low position the hand is close to the drumhead, so you are able to hit the drum before lifting the hand higher. In the high position, the hand is situated higher and will need to travel down towards the drum in order to hit the drumhead.

Understanding the basic strokes will significantly help you when learning the techniques that will be discussed in this book. This will also help you develop solid stick control and contribute towards achieving convincing sound from the drum kit.

Full Stroke

The hand starts in the high position and finishes in the high position.

Down Stroke

The hand starts in the high position and finishes in the low position.

Up Stroke

The hand starts in the low position and finishes in the high position.

Tap Stroke

The hand starts in the low position and finishes in the low position.

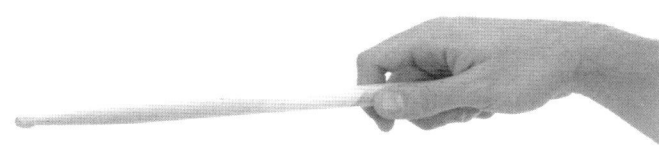

Hand position: high

Hand position: low

The Pedals

The Bass Drum

There are two main techniques for playing the bass drum pedal: heel up and heel down.

In heel down technique, you place your foot completely flat on the pedal. Ensure that your toes are not too high on the pedal board. Strike your foot down to operate the pedal. When performed correctly, it should feel that the weight of your leg and foot sits in your heel and you move from your ankle.

The heel up technique is most commonly used for power and volume. In order to try this technique place your toes on the pedal but lift your ankle so it is not touching the pedal. Keep your toes in touch with the pedal and press your leg down to operate the pedal. When performed correctly, the weight of your leg is directed into your toes and you move from your hip. Experiment with both techniques and use the one that works best for you. Professional drummers master both techniques and are able to change between them smoothly according to the musical context.

> # Tip!
>
> *You can adjust the tension of the spring in the bass drum pedal and even the distance of the beater from the bass drumhead. This will help you achieve the most comfortable position according to your technique and therefore quickly develop reliable bass drum control.*

Heel Down Technique before playing the bass drum

Heel Up Technique before playing the bass drum

Heel Down Technique after playing the bass drum

Heel Up Technique after playing the bass drum

The Hi-Hat

The hi-hat pedal can also be played with the two techniques discussed opposite.

As with the bass drum, the heel up technique will produce a more powerful and snappy sound.

The hi-hat can be played in two main positions: the closed hi-hat and the open hi-hat.

When playing the closed hi-hat, strike the hi-hat while holding down the pedal tightly with your foot. In order to create the open hi-hat sound you will need to loosen the hi-hat pedal and allow the top hi-hat cymbal to come up just before striking it. Mastering the exact timing of when to open and close the hi-hat can take time but is crucial for every drummer.

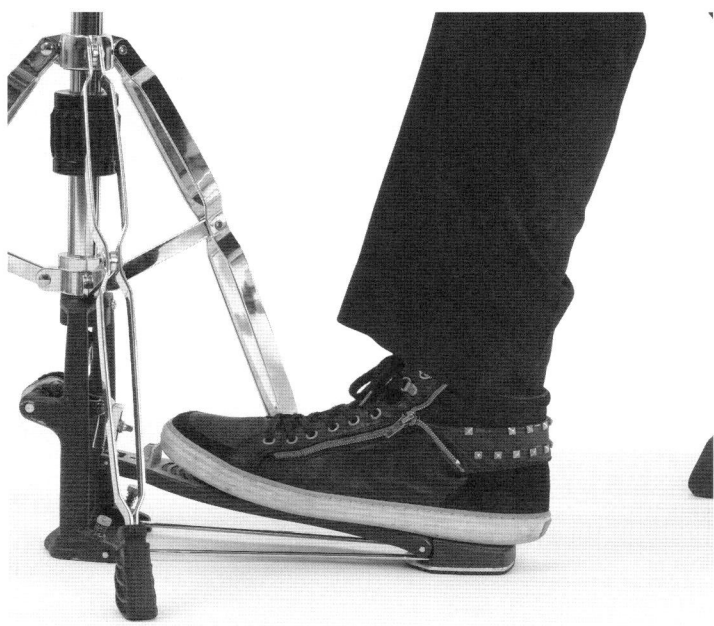

Hi-Hat: Heel Down Technique

Closed Hi-Hat

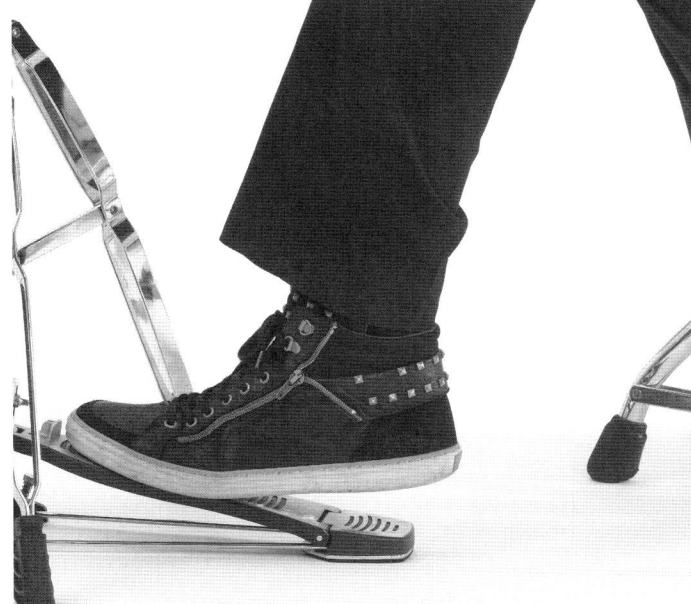

Hi-Hat: Heel Up Technique

Open Hi-Hat

Drum Notation

All the notation that will be used in this book is detailed below. Feel free to refer back to this page at any point.

Drums

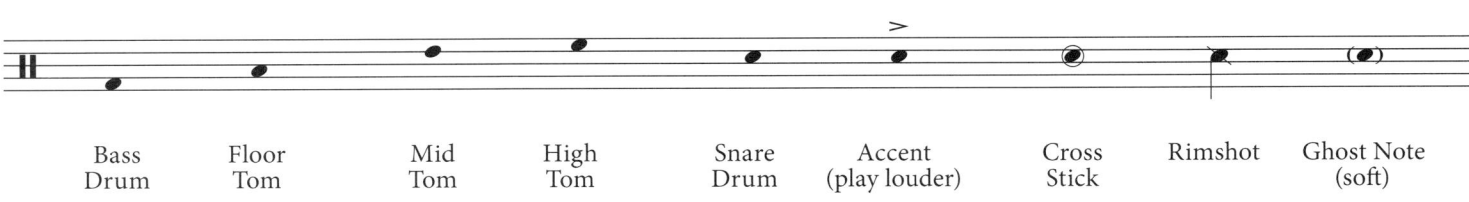

| Bass Drum | Floor Tom | Mid Tom | High Tom | Snare Drum | Accent (play louder) | Cross Stick | Rimshot | Ghost Note (soft) |

Cymbals

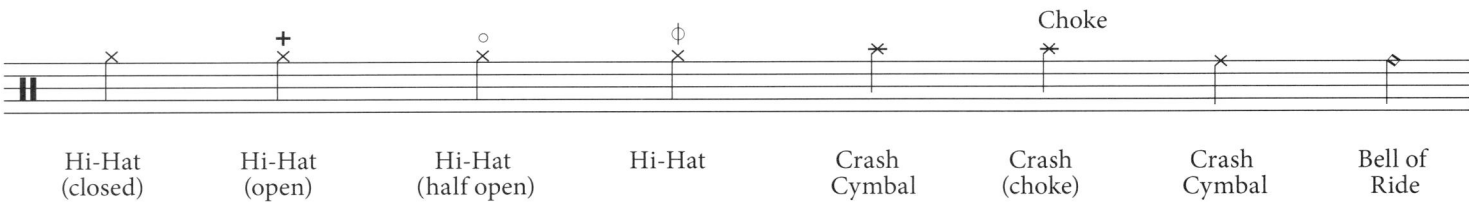

| Hi-Hat (closed) | Hi-Hat (open) | Hi-Hat (half open) | Hi-Hat | Crash Cymbal | Crash (choke) | Crash Cymbal | Bell of Ride |

Note & Rest Values

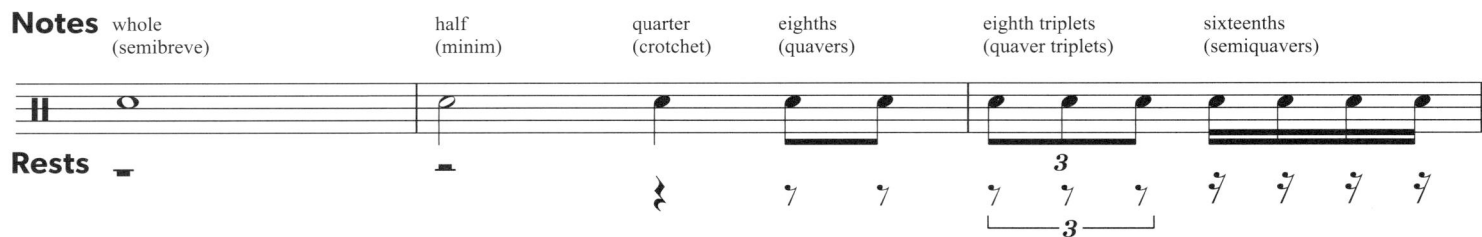

Notes whole (semibreve) · half (minim) · quarter (crotchet) · eighths (quavers) · eighth triplets (quaver triplets) · sixteenths (semiquavers)

Rests

Musical Structure

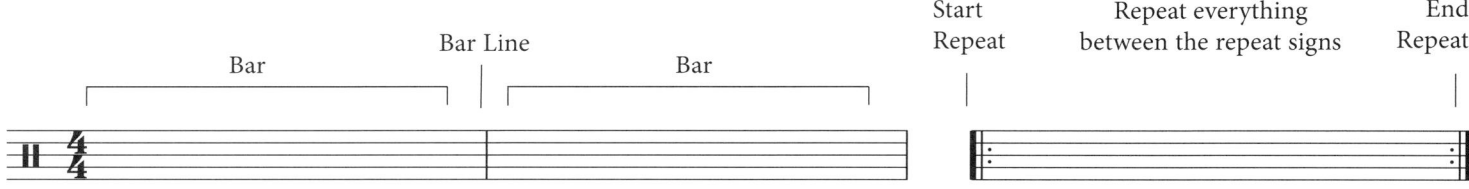

Bar · Bar Line · Bar

Start Repeat · Repeat everything between the repeat signs · End Repeat

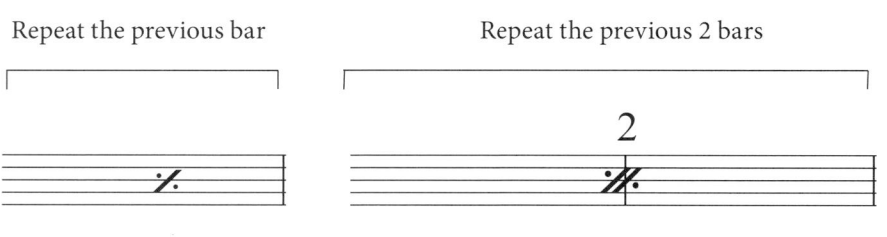

Repeat the previous bar

Repeat the previous 2 bars

First & second time bars:
Play the first time bar, repeat from start repeat, then go straight to the second time bar (miss the first time bar)

1.   2.

D.C. al Coda - Go back to the beginning and follow the To Coda sign

D.S. al Coda – Go back to the 𝄋 sign and follow the To Coda sign

Time signature: Top number indicates the number of beats per bar. Bottom number shows the note type used for each beat (e.g. 4/4 means 4 quarter notes per bar)

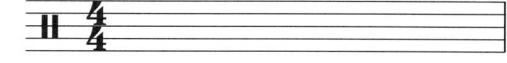

Dynamics

Dynamics

Dynamics symbols tell us how loudly or quietly to play, using the letters *p* and *f* :

p *f*
piano forte
(soft) (loud)

These may be doubled or tripled for greater effect:

pp *ff*
pianissimo fortissimo
(very soft) (very loud)

ppp *fff*
pianississimo fortissississimo
(very very soft) (very very loud)

The prefix *m* stands for *mezzo* (moderately)

mp *mf*
mezzopiano mezzoforte
(moderately (moderately
soft) loud)

Dynamics are always relative – 'very soft' at performance volume could be louder than 'very loud' at practice volume. Playing softly on the drums is much harder than playing loudly but developing the ability to play softly is very important for every musician.

Getting Louder

In rock and pop music, dynamics instructions are often used to tell you to get gradually louder *(crescendo)* or softer *(diminuendo)*. This is either shown using abbreviations of these words:

cresc. gradually becoming louder

dim. gradually becoming softer

Or 'hairpin' symbols:

gradually becoming louder

gradually becoming softer

It is important to understand and practise the concept of dynamics on the drum kit from the beginning. Playing an instrument with dynamic changes adds a layer of musicality and helps you develop your sensitivity and touch which in the long run help you develop your own sound.

Sound Production and Balance

Hitting the drums in the middle with secure technique will help you achieve a solid sound from the kit. It is also important to learn how to balance the parts of the kit as this is one of the factors in achieving a solid groove. The ideal balance between kit parts will change according to the music played and instrument used. For example, if you are playing rock the bass drum and snare should be louder than the hi-hat. However, if you are playing jazz the ride cymbal and hi-hat should be louder than the bass drum and snare.

Introduction to Sight Reading

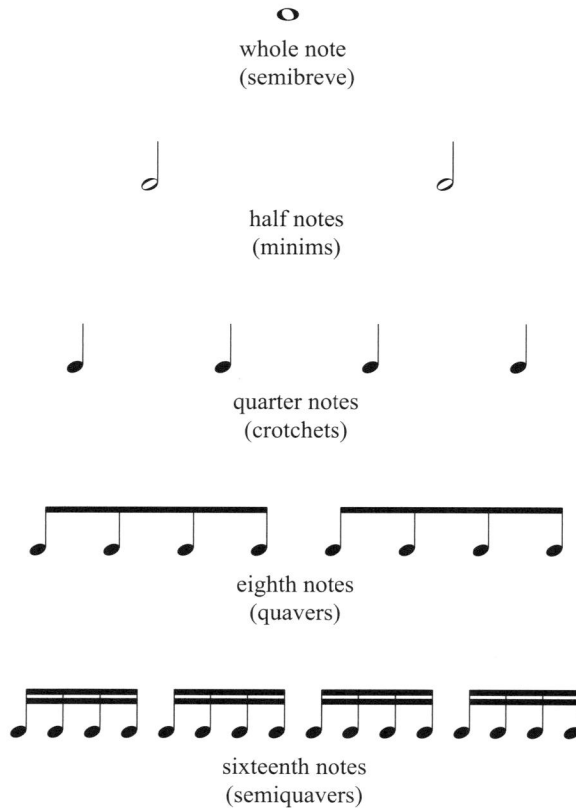

whole note
(semibreve)

half notes
(minims)

quarter notes
(crotchets)

eighth notes
(quavers)

sixteenth notes
(semiquavers)

A whole note (or semibreve) lasts four full beats.
It is counted as 1 2 3 4.

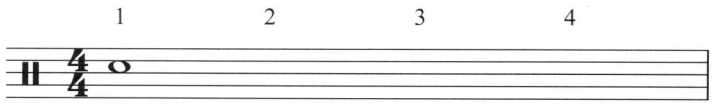

A half note (or minim) lasts two full beats.
It is counted as 1 2 or 3 4.

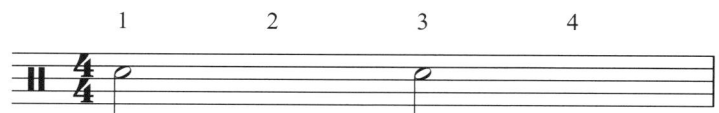

A quarter note (or crotchet) lasts for one full beat.
Four quarter note beats are counted as 1 2 3 4.

An eighth note (or quaver) lasts half a beat.
A full bar of eighth notes is counted as 1 & 2 & 3 & 4 &.

A sixteenth note (or semiquaver) lasts a quarter of a
beat. A full bar of sixteenth notes is counted as 1 e & a
2 e & a 3 e & a 4 e & a.

Tip!

*Counting the beats while practising is
an excellent way to develop your sense of time
and understanding of the pulse.*

The Metronome

The metronome is an exceptionally useful tool for drummers. This device produces a regular 'click' sound. The speed ('tempo') can easily be adjusted, and is measured in beats per minute – often abbreviated to bpm. Most digital metronomes can easily be set to play various rhythms: this can be particularly helpful when practising new note values. If you own a smartphone or a tablet there are many metronome apps that you might want to try too.

Consistent practice with a metronome will help you develop your sense of time. This means that you will be able to keep a steady pulse even when playing without the metronome. This is one of the most important roles of a drummer in a band, so if you can start developing this skill from the beginning, you should become very sought-after by bands around you.

A digital metronome

Internal Clock

The main role of the drummer in a band is keeping a consistent pulse while playing stylistic grooves and fills. Therefore understanding this concept and developing an inner sense of time is crucial, even from the very early stages. This inner sense of time is often referred to as internal clock in the drumming world.

Playing consistent patterns with a metronome or suitable backing tracks is the best way of developing secure time, accuracy and muscle memory. Playing without a metronome or music is also important, as it will give you an indication of how steadily you can keep the beat yourself. If you have the facilities, record yourself drumming whenever possible and listen back in order to progress.

As you continue to develop as a drummer, you will probably start playing with other musicians before long. Remember that although you are supposed to keep the pulse consistent, it is also important to listen to the other musicians and ensure that you are playing with them and not only focusing on the pulse.

In this book you will learn how to play drum grooves in many styles of music. In some of these styles, the drummer is actually expected not to groove like a metronome but slightly looser. Therefore keeping your ears tuned to the other musicians is key. Developing your listening skills together with a solid internal clock will lead to reliable musicianship throughout your technical progress.

The Basic Rhythms

In the exercises below you will learn some basic rhythms. All exercises are notated on the snare drum.

1

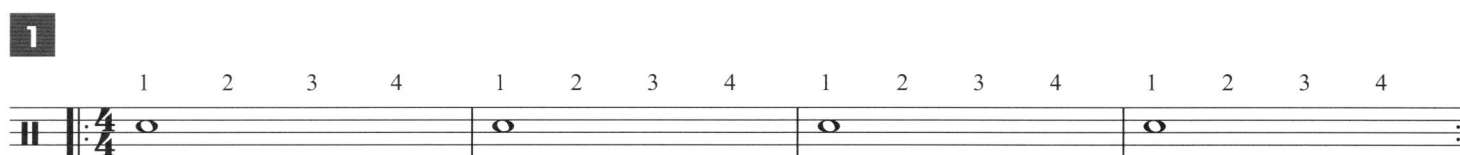

This is the whole note rest: —▪— This means that there is nothing to play for four beats. However you still need to count the full four beats during this rest.

2

3

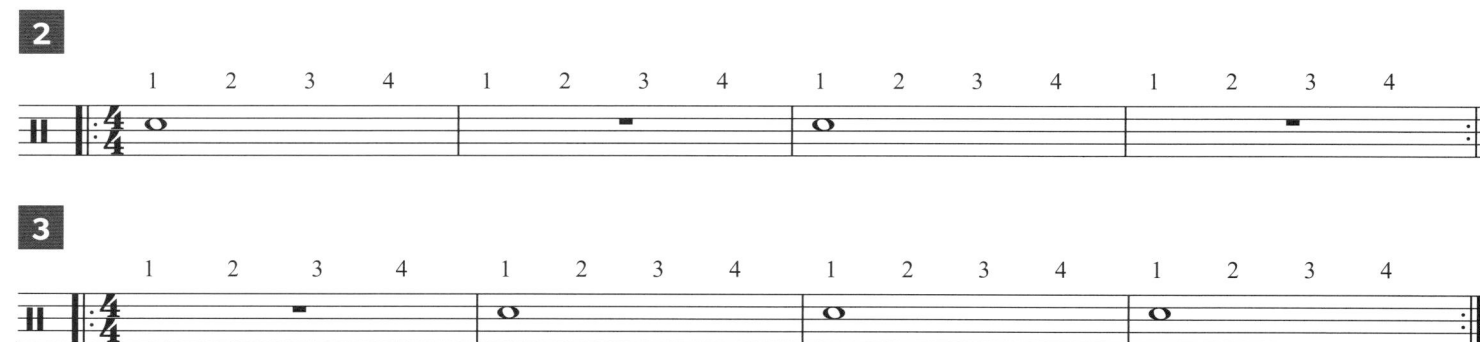

Now let's practise some half notes on the snare. Use alternate sticking (R L R L if you are right-handed, L R L R if you are left-handed) and keep counting the beats throughout.

In order to develop your technique and coordination with balance it is very important that you practise everything starting with both hands. This applies to reading exercises, rudiments, grooves, fills and anything else that has suggested sticking throughout this series.

4

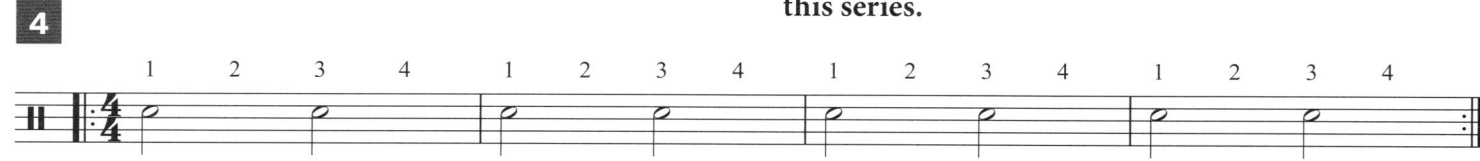

This is the half note rest: —▪— This means that there is nothing to play for two beats. However you still need to count the full two beats during this rest.

5

6

The next rhythm we will play on the snare is the quarter note rhythm.
This means that there is one note on each beat

1

This is the quarter note rest: ╶𝄽╴ This means that there is nothing to play for one beat. However you still need to count a full beat during this rest.

Exercises 2–6 should be played with alternate sticking. Aim to keep the pulse consistent and remember that a metronome can be very helpful with this.

2

3

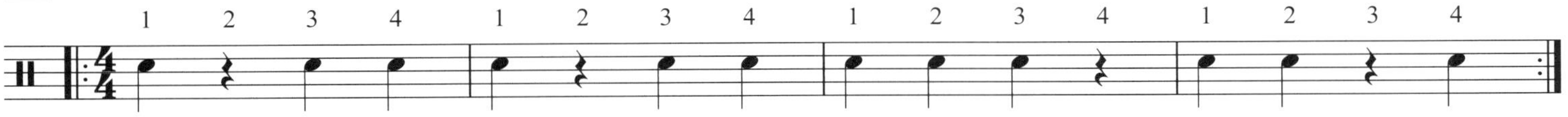

4

5

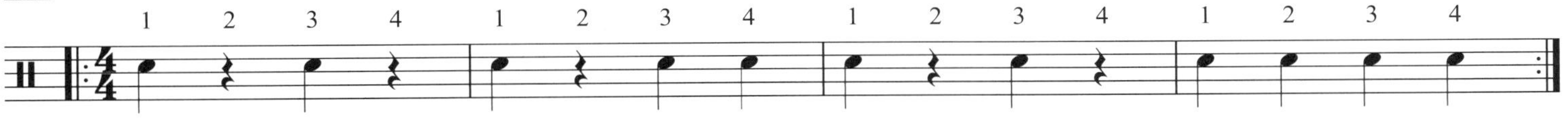

6

Tip!

If you want to push yourself try practising the exercises above in the following way –
this will significantly help you develop your hands coordination:
1 *Right hand plays the written exercise and left hand plays consistent quarter notes throughout.*
2 *Left hand plays the written exercise and right hand plays quarter notes throughout.*
The hands can play the same drum or a combination of the snare drum and toms.

Introduction to Rudiments

Singles, Doubles, Paradiddles

The foundation of drumming is based on three basic sticking patterns: singles, doubles and paradiddles as well as unisons (two or more notes played at the same time). The exercises (rudiments) below are written in quarter notes; the counting is not indicated so remember to count 1 2 3 4. Practise these three exercises on the snare drum at various speeds.

Aim to play even strokes and produce a balanced sound from the drum. Gradually build up the speed of the exercises without compromising the sound and experiment with moving the hands around the drum kit. The letters above the notation will remind you which hand to use. If you are a left-handed drummer make sure to reverse the sticking.

Single Strokes in Quarter Notes

Double Strokes in Quarter Notes

Paradiddles in Quarter Notes

Practice Pads

Many drummers use practice pads in order to develop solid technique and stick control. These pads bounce like a snare drum but don't make much noise. If your neighbours complain about the noise you make while playing the drums, you can get a whole set of practice pads that will fit your acoustic drum kit.

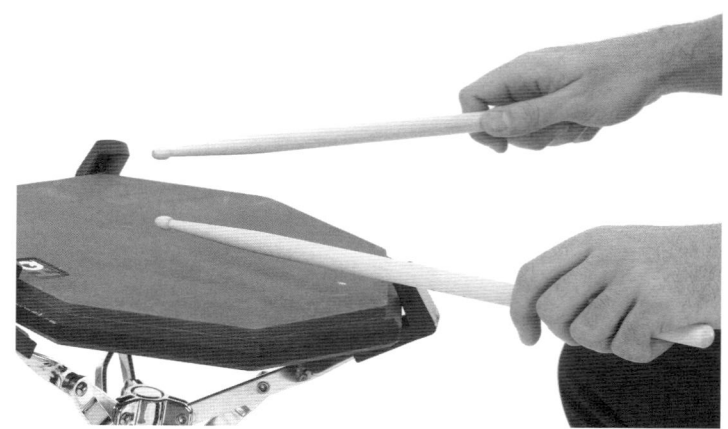

Eighth Notes

The basic rudiments shown on the previous page can be played in any rhythm. Let's try to play them again using a new rhythm: eighth notes. As shown on p. 18, eighth notes are counted as 1 & 2 & 3 & 4 &. Most of the drum beats in this book are constructed from eighth notes and quarter notes. Practise the following exercises with a metronome; when you feel comfortable, raise the tempo gradually. Remember that it is crucial to reverse the sticking in order to strengthen both hands equally.

Single Strokes in Eighth Notes

Double Strokes in Eighth Notes

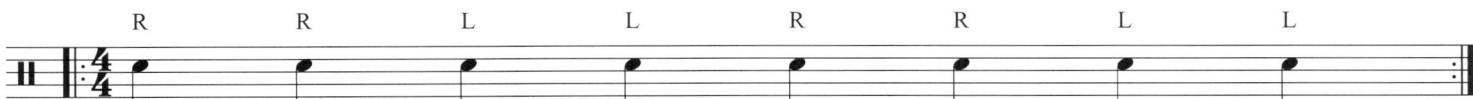

Paradiddles in Eighth Notes

These exercises can also be played with various feet patterns. The two drum voices we will use are the bass drum and hi-hat foot (playing the hi-hat with the foot only, not the hands). When you have mastered the exercises below try to create your own exercises from the rudiments and feet patterns shown on this page.

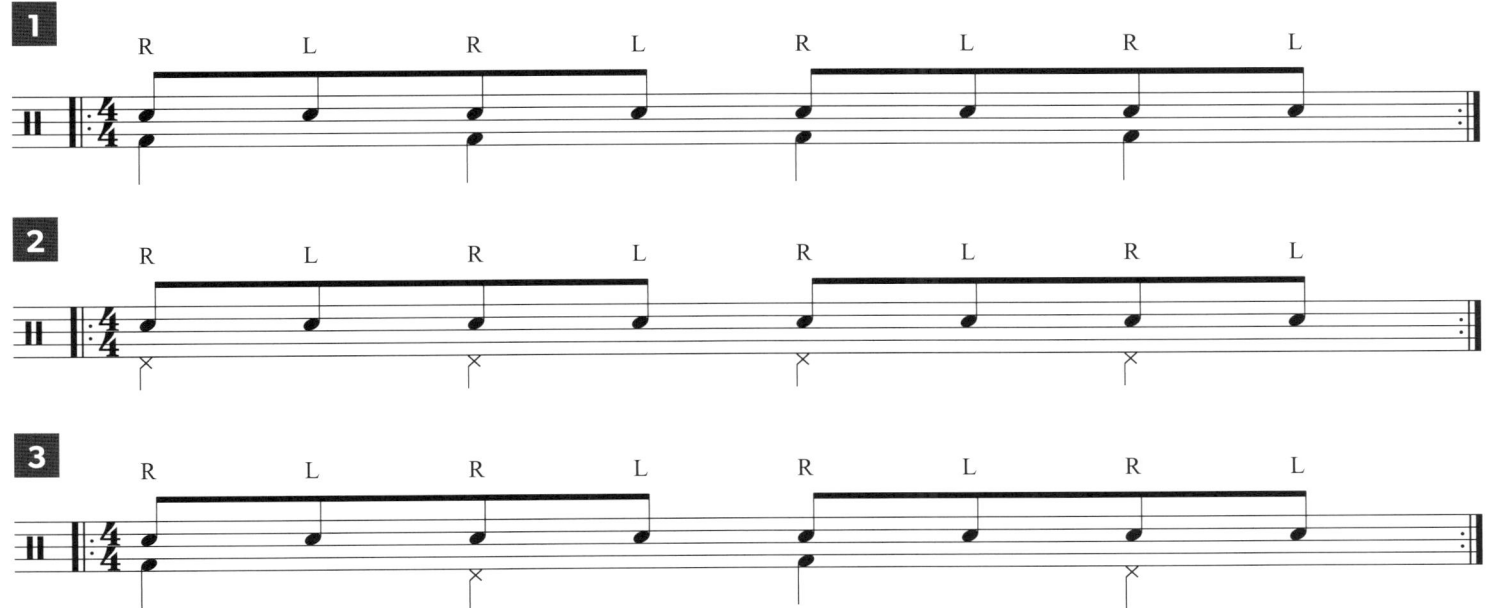

Sight Reading

The exercises on these pages will give you the drumming vocabulary needed for this level. If you find these very challenging, try using them like short studies: break down each exercise into individual bars and practise each bar with a metronome until it feels comfortable. When you feel ready put the four bar phrase together and even try it at faster tempos. You can use any sticking combination – experiment and find the most comfortable and natural combinations. The counting above the notes is only shown in the first exercise. Try to write down the counting of all the other exercises before playing them. Follow this system with all other exercises in this book where the counting is not provided: this will ensure that you fully understand the rhythms used and help you prepare for similar sections in any grade exam.

Adding Rests

Now let's add quarter note rests to these 4-bar phrases.

1

2

3

4

5

6

Grooves: Eighth Note Rock

The drum beats below (also known as grooves) are generally the most basic eighth note grooves that are used in rock and pop music. Notice that the hi-hat plays consistent eighth notes throughout. The snare drum plays mainly on the *backbeat*: the second and fourth beats of the bar in a $\frac{4}{4}$ groove. The bass drum pattern varies slightly in each example, but is mainly used to strengthen the first and third beats of each bar.

Practise the beats at a slow tempo and increase the speed gradually when you feel comfortable. Remember that the hi-hat is closed throughout these grooves. A common way of practising new grooves is starting with one drum voice (for example the hi-hat) and adding one drum voice at a time until you can play the full groove comfortably. You may want to use a metronome to help you keep the pulse consistent.

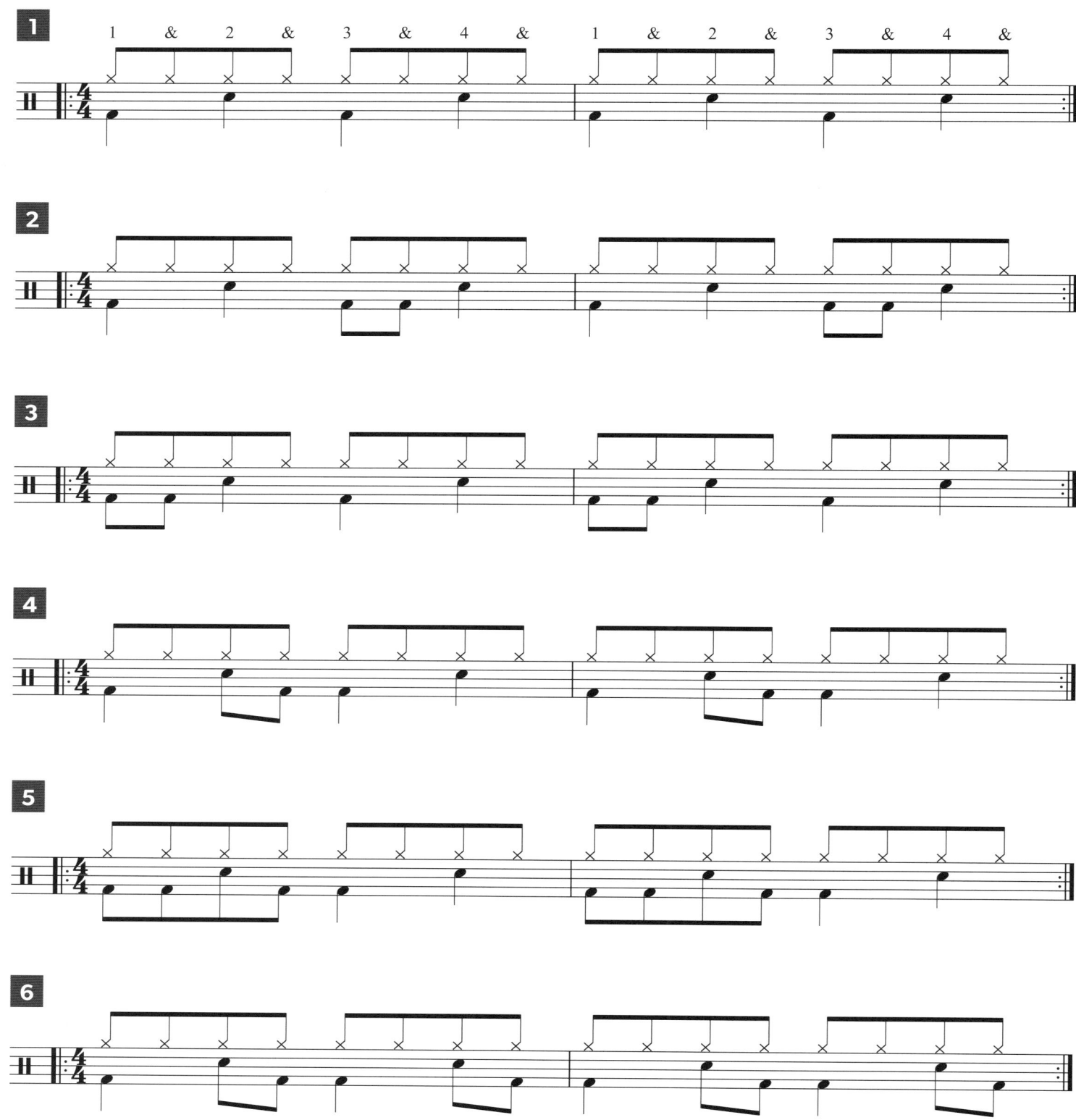

In these examples the hi-hat pattern remains as on p. 26 but there are variations in the snare drum part as well as some quarter note rests. Practise these grooves and remember these important points:

- You are aiming to produce consistent sound from each part of the drum kit as well as a balanced kit sound overall.

- Practising with a metronome or music will help you keep the pulse consistent.

- Counting aloud while practising will help develop your internal clock and help you recognise any errors.

- If you practise the grooves consistently and maintain a relaxed posture your technique, coordination and sense of time will continue to improve.

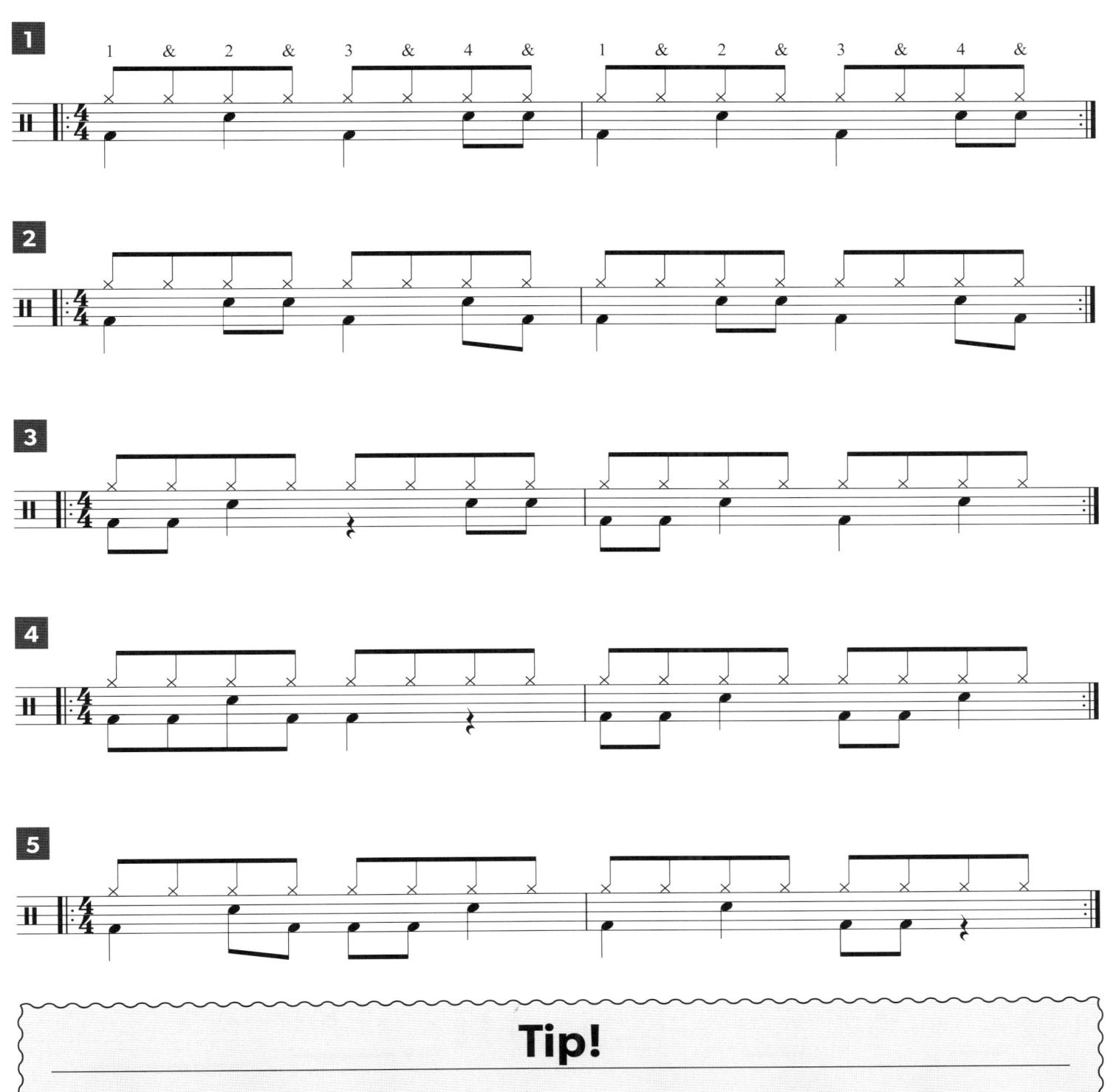

Tip!

It is important to practise your grooves every day at consistent speed. Therefore, you may want to choose music that you really like at various speeds to play along to. When you listen to your favourite tracks, try to identify the grooves being played. This will help you to start developing your ear.

Drum Fills

Fills or drum fills are rhythmic phrases that are played by the drummer when not playing a groove. These usually signify a musical change, or the beginning or end of a section in a song.

Let's practise some ideas first: practise each one of these fills repeatedly and use a metronome to keep the pulse consistent.

1

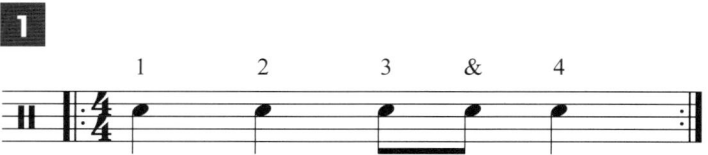

2

3

4

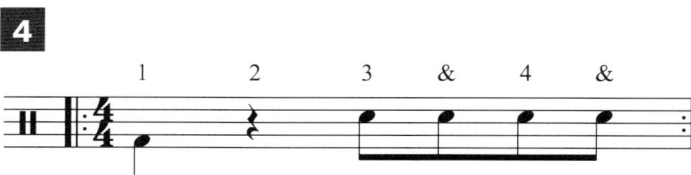

5

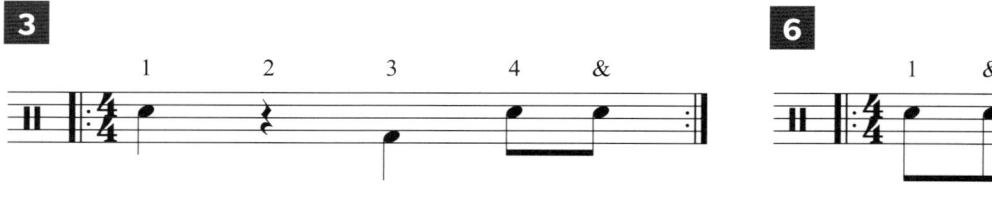

6

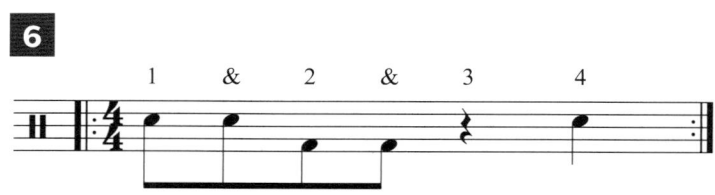

The following six fills use the same rhythms used above on the snare, high tom, mid tom, floor tom and bass drum. If you need to remind yourself where these are notated, please refer to the notation guide on p. 16. When playing a fill it is important to plan the sticking that you want to use. Generally, drummers tend to start a fill with the leading hand (R if right-handed,

L if left-handed) and follow a logical alternation sequence that feels comfortable. It is recommended that you spend some time, experiment and find the sticking pattern that suits your technique best. When you feel comfortable with these fills, try playing them again but start with your following hand. This will strengthen this hand and help build up its technique.

7

8

9

10

11

12

Now let's combine fills with some of the grooves learned earlier in this book. The eighth note groove in the first bar of each exercise will be played three times, then in the fourth there is a drum fill. Once y... able to play these exercises, put on your favou... ...ock or pop music and use them to play along.

Tip!

These fills were written for the classic five-piece drum kit setup (bass drum, snare, high tom, mid tom and floor tom). If you are using a four-piece drum kit, this will usually mean that you are using a high tom and a floor tom. The mid tom strokes can be assigned to either one of these toms.

sing the Cymbals

In these exercises you will learn how to add the crash cymbal to a basic rock groove.

Hit the crash with conviction and aim for fluent and consistent movement between the crash cymbal and other parts of the kit. After hitting the crash cymbal, let the stick bounce back naturally to avoid 'choking' the sound.

Although the crash can be played with either the right or left hand, most drummers tend to hit their main crash cymbal with their leading hand (the right hand, if you are a right-handed drummer).

1

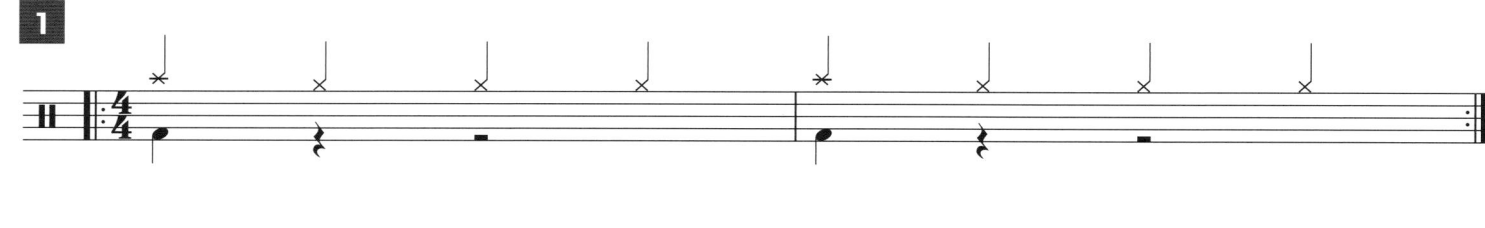

2

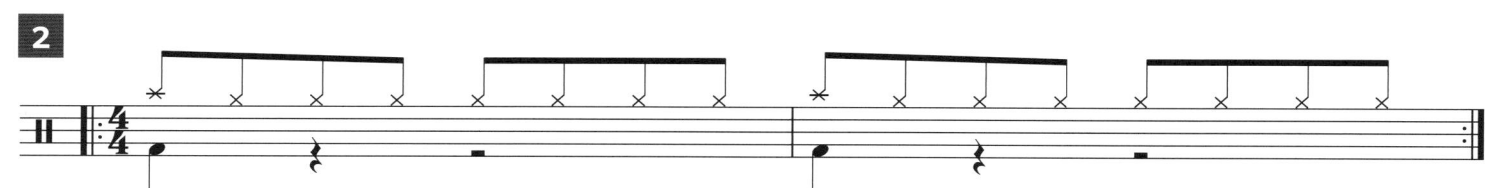

The ride cymbal has various roles in drumming, however the most common role is playing the main cymbal pattern in a groove instead of the hi-hat. Finding a comfortable hand position and keeping the ride cymbal sound consistent will be the initial issues to deal with. Try playing the grooves from p. 26-27, replacing the hi-hat pattern with the ride cymbal patterns from **Ex. 3** and **Ex. 4** below.

Tip!

If you do not have a crash cymbal in your setup, you can play the cymbal hits on the ride cymbal but be sure to use the neck of the stick on the edge of the cymbal in order achieve the 'crash' sound.

3

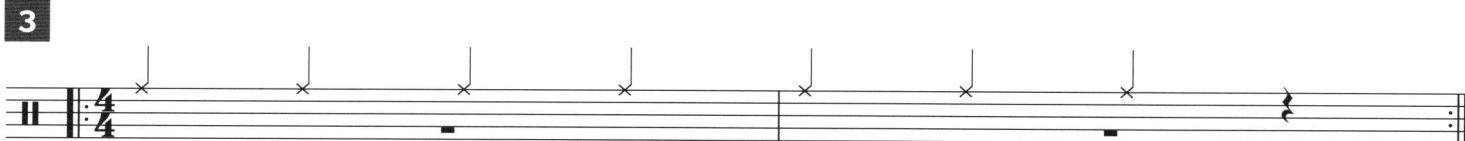

4

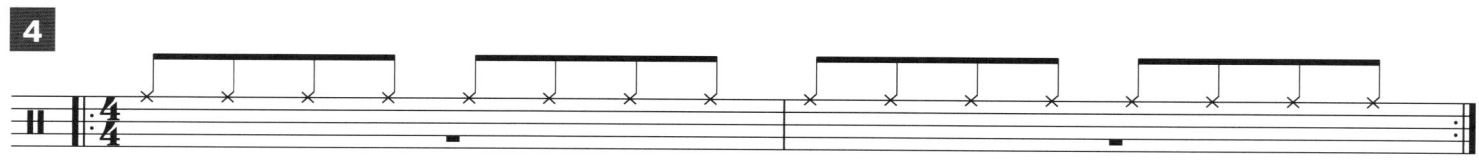

5

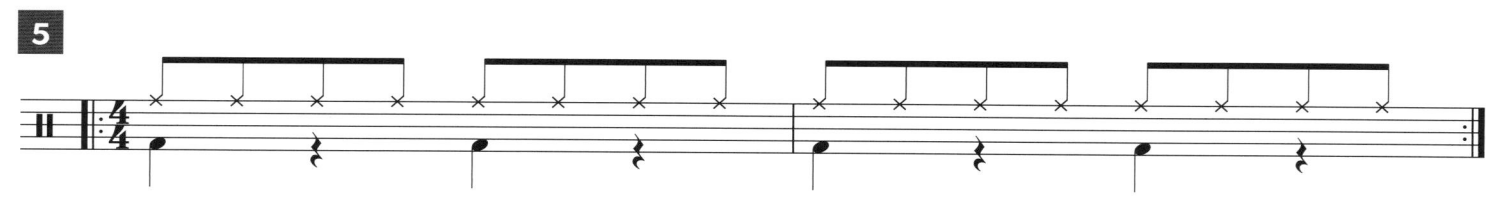

The Open Hi-Hat

The open hi-hat is an important technique that you will need to master in this early stage of your drumming career. Please refer to p. 15 for a breakdown of this specific technique. Focus on achieving the right sound, timing, consistency of the pulse and keeping your posture balanced. The open hi-hat is effective in any style of music, so practise the exercises below slowly in order to develop accurate timing of this technique. Exercises 4–6 combine the open hi-hat with the ride and crash cymbals. When you feel comfortable with these patterns try combining them with grooves and fills that you already know.

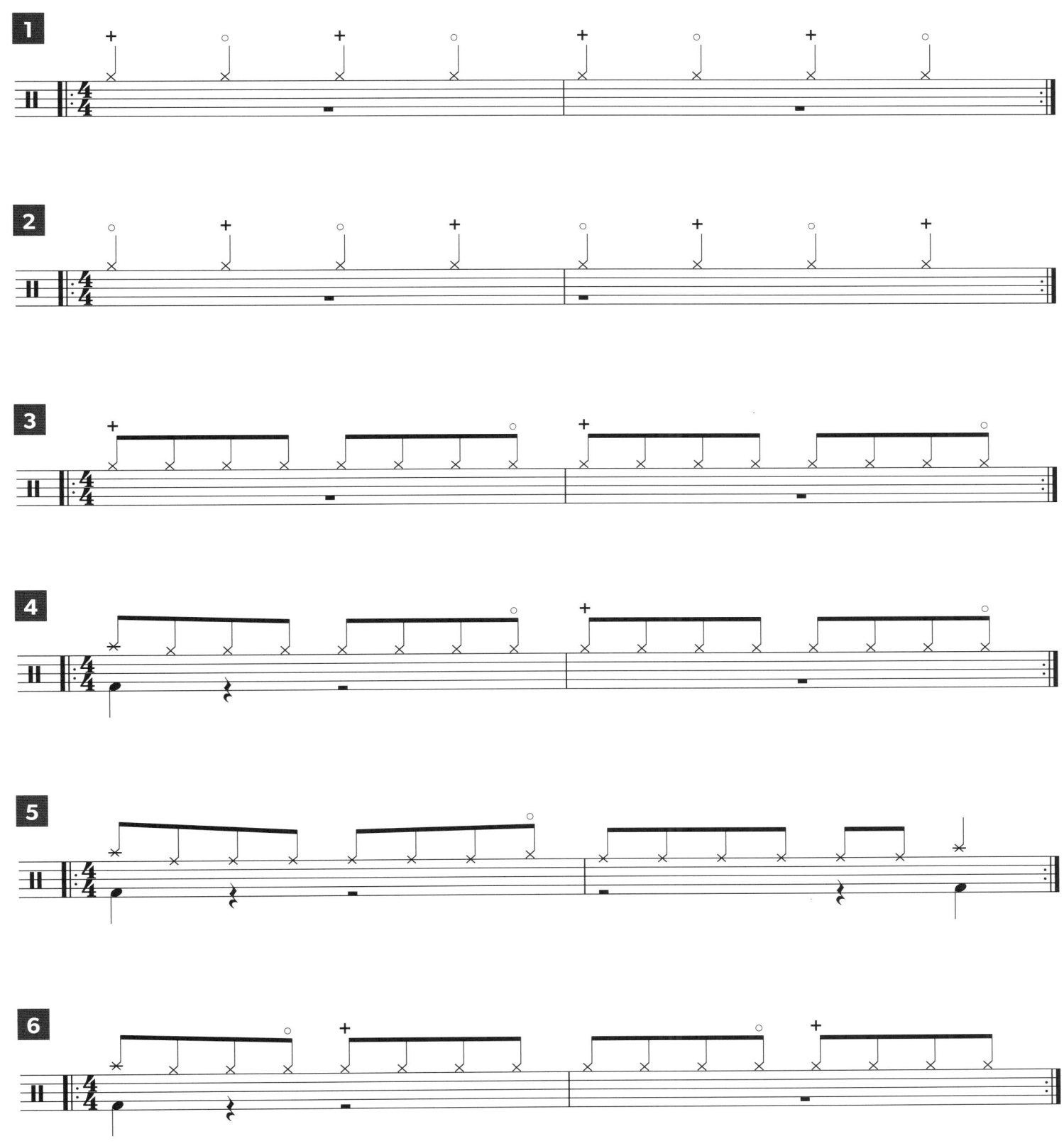

Rhythms: Sixteenth Notes

In this section you will learn to use a new rhythm: sixteenth notes.

These are equal to a quarter of a beat and are counted as '1 e & a 2 e & a 3 e & a 4 e & a'. If you are using a digital metronome you may be able to adjust it to play sixteenth notes. The exercises below contain continuous sixteenth notes using the snare drum and toms.

Practise the exercises with alternating hands and aim to produce balanced strokes throughout. These basic ideas should be developed with various voicings in order to create your own fills.

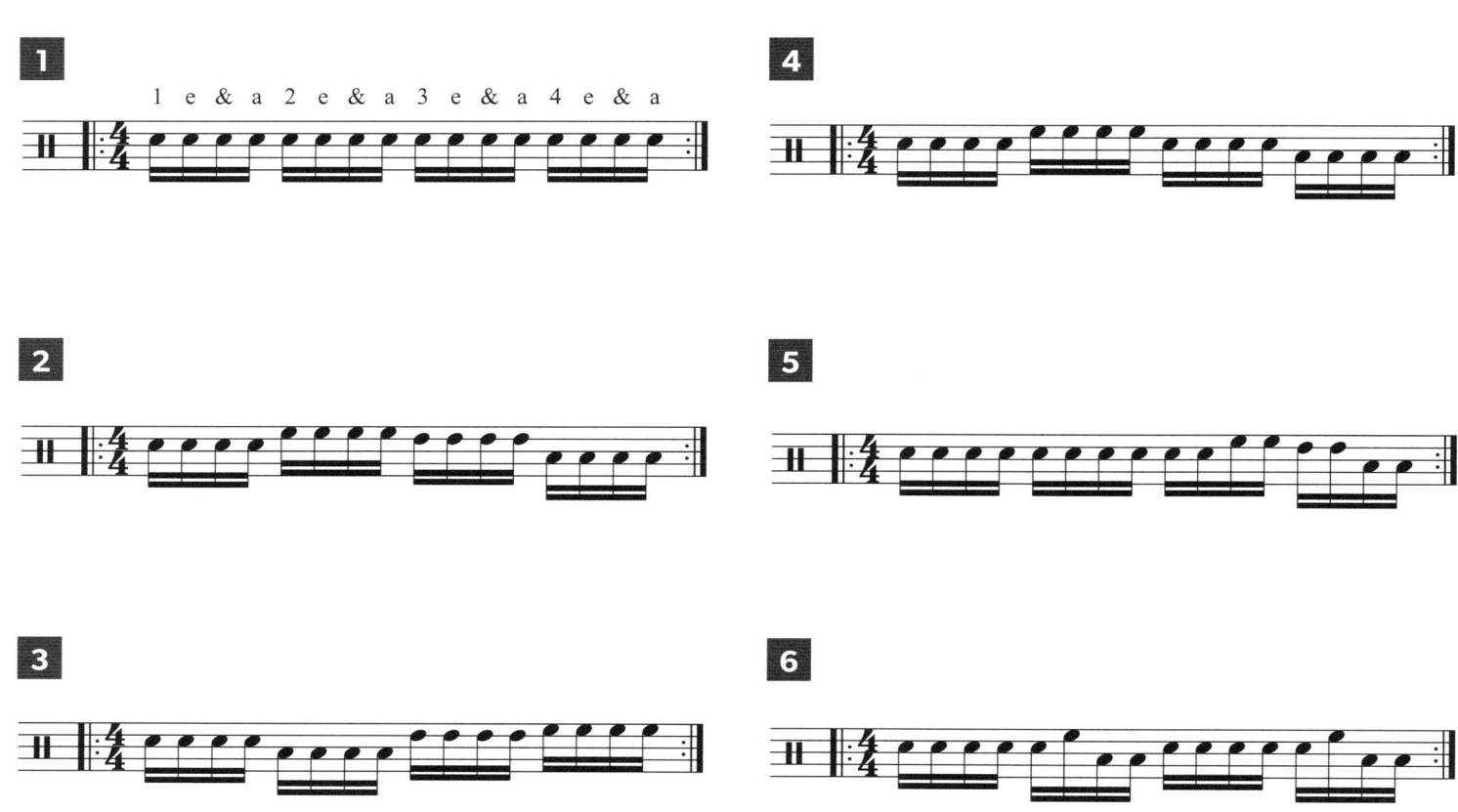

Now let's combine sixteenth notes with eighth notes and quarter notes. The rhythms in **Ex. 7** & **8** are notated on the snare drum only. Then these are shown with a suggested voicing that includes the toms in **Ex. 9** & **10**.

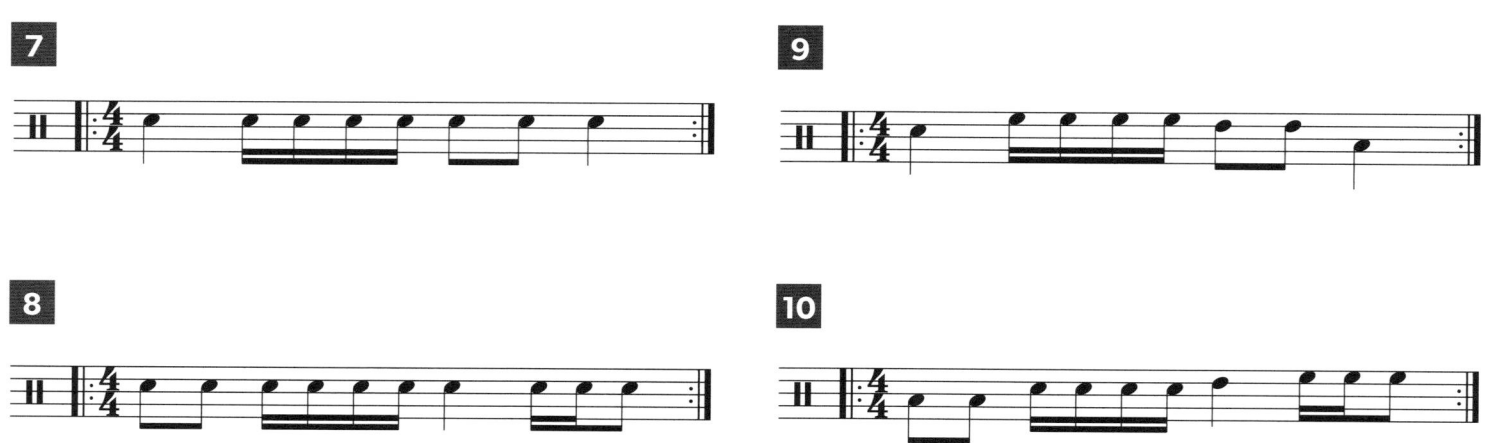

Combining Rhythms

The exercises on this page include the main three rhythms that you have learned: quarter notes, eighth notes and sixteenth notes. There are no rests in these exercises but it is crucial that you remember the length of each rhythm and use the appropriate counting.

Although the exercises are written on the snare, feel free to move them around the kit if you want to challenge yourself. The counting is marked in the exercises below. Notes that should not be played but still accounted for are marked in brackets.

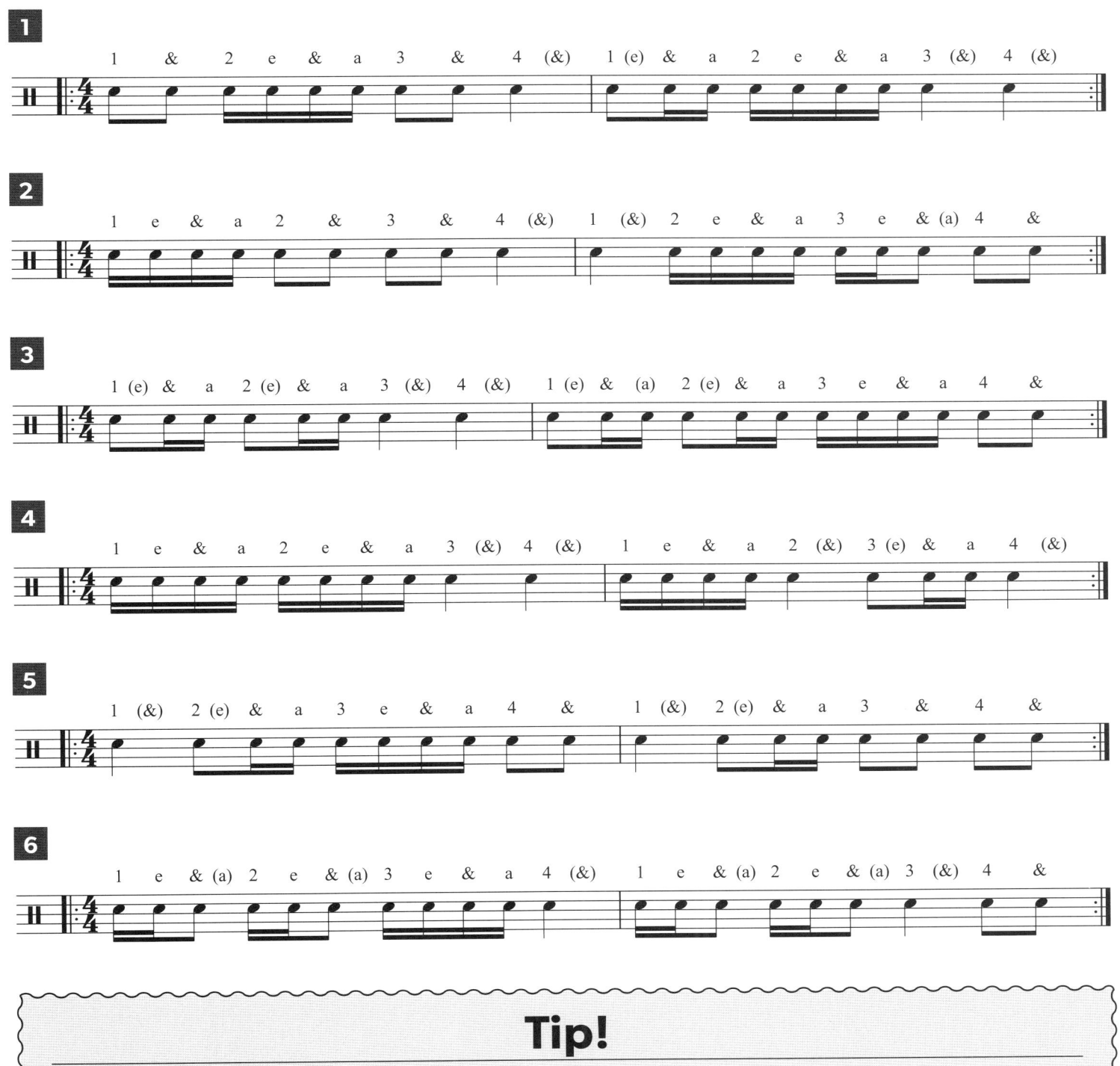

Tip!

Playing quarter note bass drums throughout these exercises will help you improve your coordination skills. If you want to strengthen your stick control try to play the exercises as written with alternating hands but use doubles every time you play a group of four sixteenth notes.

Rudiments and Technique

In this section you will learn how to use the sixteenth note rhythm when playing the fundamental drum rudiments. Speed is not the most important target, so feel free to practise as slowly as you like and raise the speed gradually.

Ensure that both hands are being raised to a similar height and the sound produced is balanced. Playing these exercises for a few minutes every day will significantly improve your technique.

The following exercises will help you strengthen your hand-foot coordination. The skill of moving two (or more) limbs with accurate timing is obviously a crucial one for every drummer. It will continue to improve as long as you consistently allocate practice time for this task. In the examples below, you will learn to

combine the sixteenth note rudiments from the top of this page with some feet patterns. The sticking is not indicated but you should practise singles, doubles and paradiddles with the three feet patterns shown. When you feel comfortable with these exercises, try to vary and create your own hand-foot coordination challenges.

Accents

You will notice that there is an accent mark above some of the notes in the following exercises. Accented notes should be played louder and feel like heavier strokes than the unaccented notes. The simplest way to create this dynamic change is to lift the hand higher when playing an accent and keep it closer to the

drumhead when performing unaccented notes. Please refer back to p. 13 and remind yourself of the four basic drum strokes that can be used. There is no need to use all these strokes during the exercises below – simply find the best stroke for each hand in order to create the accent naturally.

Now let's move the accented phrases around the kit. You will find below three variations of Exercise 1 but feel free to invent some of your own exercises as well.

Be creative and use various rhythms, voicings, rudiments and accents. Don't forget to practise Exercises 2 and 3 with movement around the kit too.

Sight Reading: Snare Drum

These sight reading exercises include the three main rhythms that you have learned as well as quarter and eighth note rests. Start by writing the counting above each exercise. Then practise the rhythms slowly and gradually increase the tempo.

The exercises are written on the snare drum but feel free to move them around the kit when you feel comfortable. Various sticking options can be used in these exercises and you should obviously choose the one that suits you best. Suggested sticking patterns are shown below as a starting point.

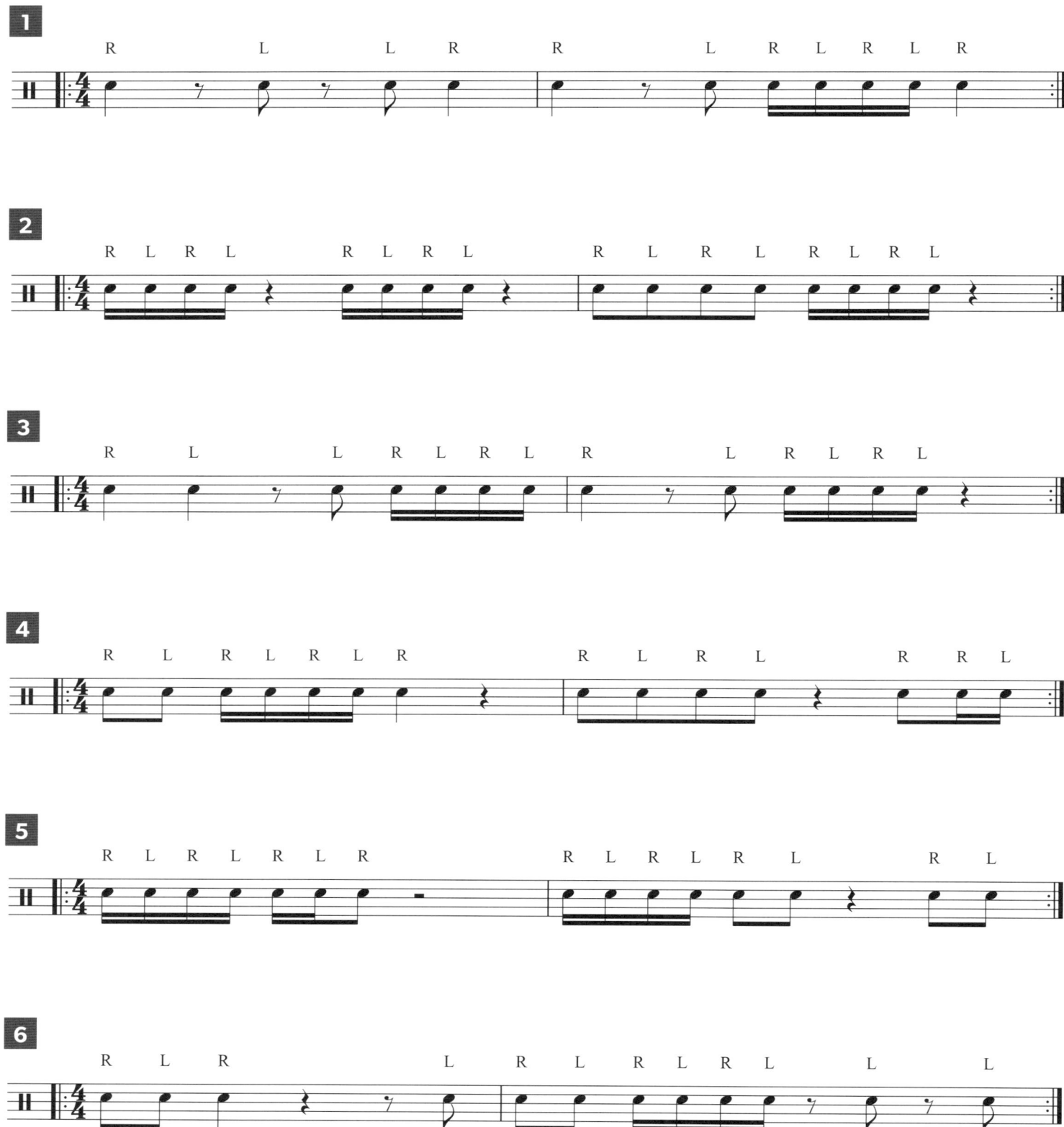

Sight Reading: Drum Kit

Now let's practise sight reading of grooves and fills using the snare, bass drum, hi-hat and toms. Ensure that after playing the drum fill you can come back into the groove while keeping the pulse consistent.

The repeat signs in the second and third bars indicate that the groove which is notated in the first bars should be repeated. However, feel free to vary the groove once you have mastered the exercise.

Grooves: Adding the Cymbals

In the following three exercises you will find ways of adding the crash cymbal into the groove.

Focus on the movement between the crash cymbal and the other parts of the drum kit. Aim for relaxed, accurate and efficient hand movement. In order to produce the best sound from your crash cymbal, try using the neck of the drumstick.

Hit the cymbal with conviction but not too loud as you might lose some of the natural character of the cymbal. Allow the stick to bounce back afterwards to avoid choking the sound.

Now let's add the ride cymbal to the groove. The ride cymbal should be played with the tip of the drumstick for maximum projection. Aim to hit the cymbal about

halfway between the centre and the edge. Remember that the ride cymbal should be softer than the bass drum and/or snare in this type of groove.

Grooves: Adding the Open Hi-Hat

In this section you will find two bar grooves with various open hi-hat patterns. Take your time and practise at a slow tempo: this will help you develop this technique without compromising your posture.

When you feel comfortable with these exercises, create some of your own variations in order to challenge yourself.

Now let's add the crash and ride cymbals to the grooves with the open hi-hat. When you feel comfortable with these exercises try playing them

continuously (play each exercise for four bars and move to the next without stopping).

Drum Fills and Improvisation

In this section you will learn how to play drum fills using the whole drum kit.

Practise each fill continuously until it feels even and consistent. Use the metronome in order to ensure that all the rhythms are accurate.

Use the sticking and hand movement that suits your technique best and remember to stay relaxed.

Now let's put some of these fills into four-bar sequences. Play the grooves for three consecutive bars and then play the notated fill. Repeat this many times

until you achieve consistent pulse and balanced sound. When you feel confident, try mixing up grooves, fills and voicings that you have already learned.

Improvisation

The skill of inventing and creating your own drum parts is generally referred to as *improvisation*. By now you probably already have some specific grooves and fills that you really like. In this section you will have the opportunity to write them down and understand how to improvise.

In Exercises 1–3 you should create your own bass drum and snare patterns (bars 1–3 of each exercise) as well as improvising a fill in the fourth bar. The slashed lines in the fourth bars indicate the number of beats that the improvised fill should last for.

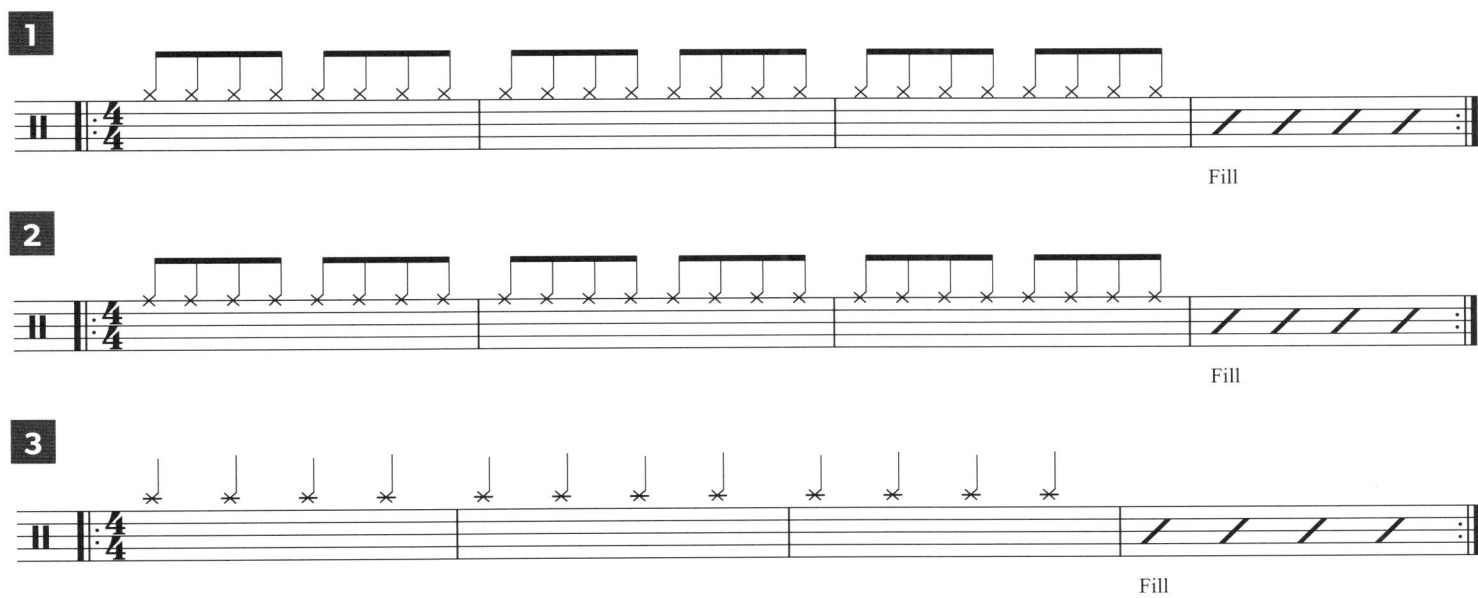

In the following three exercises you need to create your own cymbals pattern and improvise a fill. The notated bass drum and snare patterns should be played as written.

In these exercises the improvised fills should only last for two quarter note beats.

Ear Training ▶↘

▶↘ *Get these audio tracks for free from* **vvinner.com/downloads**

In this section you will learn about some of the most important aural skills that you should develop as a drummer.

The suggested exercises here will be a good starting point and should inspire you to continue to improve your aural skills and musicianship. If you are planning to take a grade exam, bear in mind that every examination board has their own method of examining your aural abilities – therefore it is crucial to familiarise yourself with their specifications and prepare accordingly.

Play each audio track without looking at the examples below. After a count-in of four clicks, the two-bar backing is played four times. For the first and third times, listen to the recorded drums. For the second and fourth times, try to play back what you heard. Finally, refer to the notation below to check whether you recognised the time signature, played back the exercise accurately and understand how it is written.

Rhythms

1　♩= 70　*This is the tempo marking. It indicates that the speed of this exercise is 70bpm (beats per minute).*

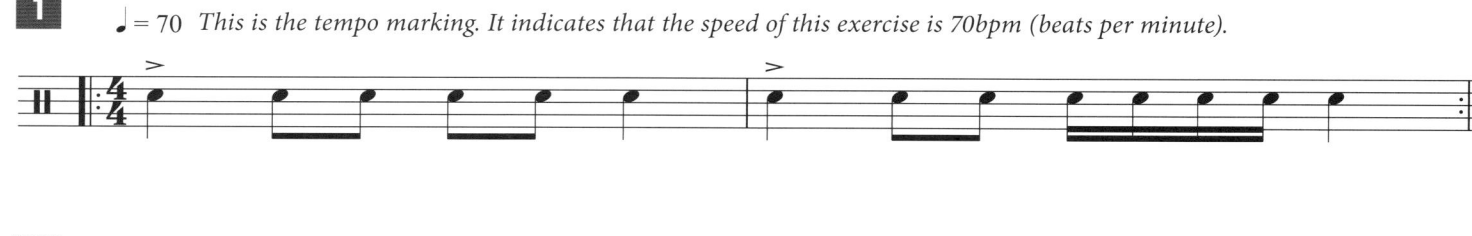

2　♩= 70

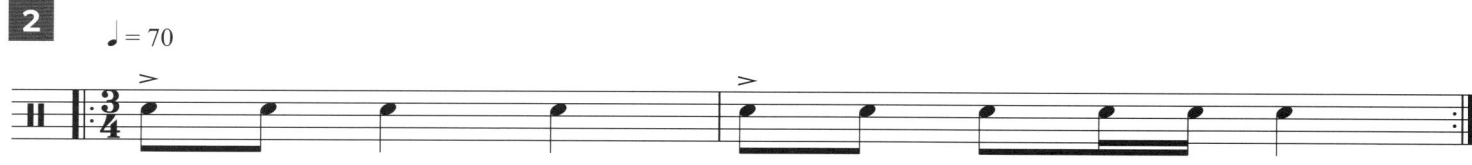

The time signature in this exercise indicates that there are 3 quarter beats in each bar. You can find more information about time signatures in P47 of this book.

Follow the same practice method with the following three examples but note that the phrases are to be played on the snare and bass drum. Count the beats throughout in order to determine the time signature.

3　♩= 70

4　♩= 70

Grooves

You will notice that Exercises 1–3 are groove based. This means that more parts of the drum kit will be used. This requires secure aural understanding as you will not only have to recognise the rhythms but also the drum voices that are being played. As explained previously, the backing track will play four times and you should attempt to play back during the second and fourth plays. The time signature on this page remains $\frac{4}{4}$, but feel free to create your own exercises in other time signatures too.

In the last three exercises of this section, there are grooves and fills. Focus on the drum voices that are being used, the rhythms and the time signature.

Practising aural skills can be a lot of fun. Follow the same method and invent some of your own exercises to help you develop further.

Inspirational Drummers

Phil Rudd

Questlove

Phil Rudd is best known for playing with the Australian hard rock band AC/DC from 1975 to 1983. His simple but effective drumming style suited the band's style of music and became an integral part of AC/DC's sound. Rudd left the band in 1983 but was asked to rejoin in 1993 and remained in the band until 2015. Since rejoining the band, he has performed on three AC/DC studio albums: *Ballbreaker*, *Stiff Upper Lip* and *Black Ice* (the band's biggest hit on the charts since *For Those About to Rock We Salute You* in 1981).

Rudd created his convincing rocky sound by using big drums and cymbals. He has mainly played Sonor drums in various sizes and Paiste cymbals. Interestingly, Rudd has only occasionally used a ride cymbal during his drumming career and has instead focused on playing his grooves on the hi-hat and large crash cymbals.

Recommended Listening

'Highway To Hell'
'Back in Black'
'Thunderstruck'

Questlove (born Ahmir Khalib Thompson) is an American drummer, DJ, music journalist and record producer best known as the drummer and frontman of the band The Roots. Questlove has also produced and worked with Jill Scott, Erykah Badu, Elvis Costello, Jay-Z, Amy Winehouse and John Legend.

As a drummer, Questlove has always provided inspiring hip hop, soul and RnB beats. He grew in popularity during the 90s and became known for his fantastic feel, ever-changing drum kits and iconic look. In 2011 Questlove was voted one of the top ten best drummers of all time by readers of *Rolling Stone* magazine.

The Roots have been the in-house band on *Late Night With Jimmy Fallon* since its première in 2009 and the *Tonight Show With Jimmy Fallon* from 2014. The band have won numerous awards throughout their career and have been described by critics as hip hop's first legitimate band.

Recommended Listening

'Web'
'Break You Off'
'How I Got Over'

Charlie Watts

The Rolling Stones in 1983. From left to right: Charlie Watts, Ronnie Wood, Keith Richards, Mick Jagger.

Charlie Watts has been the Rolling Stones' drummer since 1963. During his 50-year career with the band, he has recorded albums, toured the world and provided danceable and infectious beats for dozens of top chart hits, many of which are still popular today.

Although Watts made his name in rock, his personal tastes focus on jazz. His jazz approach to drumming made him unique in the rock world and his sound became integral to the overall sound of the band. Watts uses a simple 4-piece drum kit made by Gretsch. It includes bass drum, snare drum, floor tom and one tom. The cymbals are mainly old jazz cymbals, some of which are of unknown origin.

Apart from working with the Rolling Stones, Watts is a record producer, commercial artist and horse breeder. He has never neglected his passion for jazz music and continued to play and lead various bands over the years. In 2009 Watts toured Europe with his recent project The Charlie Watts Tentet and received the approval of many music critics.

Recommended Listening

'Sympathy For The Devil'
'Paint It Black'
'Gimme Shelter'

What Next?

Listen to records by these bands and try to understand what the drummer is doing for the music. If you like one of the drummers better than the other two, try to understand why. Is it because of their sound? Or is it their energy? Maybe it's the way they express themselves on the drum kit?

Answering these questions will help you to refine your own style and evolve as a drummer.

'Rock It!' ▶↻

The performance piece below is a summary of what we learned in the Grade 1 chapter of this book. Once you have understood and internalised the techniques, rhythms and drum voices that we used up to this point you should not find this too challenging. Be aware that there are some dynamic marks in the piece that must be addressed (refer to p. 17 for explanations of these marks). One of the main challenges will be the length of the piece (16 bars).

As with all long pieces, it is recommended to break it down: play each line (or even bar) individually and only put it together when you feel ready.

Start by practising with a metronome and build up speed until you can play with the backing track of 'Rock It!' which can be downloaded for free from **www.vvinner.com/downloads**.

Cross Stick Technique

The cross stick technique is used primarily on the snare drum.

This unique sound will be very useful in your drumming and can be used effectively in many styles of music. The cross stick is notated as a snare drum with a circle around the note head. While holding the drumstick, place the palm of your left hand on the drumhead. Then, lift it slightly in order to hit the side rim of the drum and create the cross stick sound. Ensure that you only lift the right side of your palm, not the whole hand. The left side should be used to secure the hand position by pressing the stick to the drumhead. The position of the stick on the side rim is crucial to the sound that will be achieved. Try moving the stick slightly higher, lower and also sideways until you find a sound that you like. Remember that different sticks and drums will produce slightly different sounds. When you feel comfortable with this technique feel free to add it to grooves that you have learned already.

Cross Stick: Butt Side Up

Many drummers play the cross stick with the butt side of the stick (the wider side) as it produces a louder and more convincing sound. Turn the stick around so you are gripping the neck part of the stick, adjust your position and strike the drum to produce the cross stick sound. Experiment with this and decide which way around works best for you.

Cross Stick: Tip Side Up

Time Signatures

As we have seen, the time signature indicates how many beats will be played in each bar and what type of note represents one beat. Most popular music is written in $\frac{4}{4}$, which is also referred to as *common time* in music theory. Therefore this book will largely focus on grooves and exercises in $\frac{4}{4}$.

However, developing an understanding of different time signatures, also known as odd time signatures, and the ability to recognise what time signature is being used are very important skills for every drummer. For this reason we have included some rhythmic phrases and grooves in various time signatures throughout this book.

Playing grooves in odd time signatures will strengthen your sense of time and make you a better overall musician.

If you feel that drumming in odd time signatures inspires you, there are certain styles of music that require this specific musicianship skill. We will introduce some of the iconic odd time signature drummers in higher grades of this series.

Rhythms: Triplets

The new rhythm that you will learn in this section is the eighth note triplet.

This rhythm indicates that three even notes should be played in the time of one quarter note. Triplets are most commonly counted as 1-trip-let 2-trip-let 3-trip-let 4-trip-let. Set the metronome to a comfortable tempo such as 60 bpm and try counting the triplet rhythm out loud. Ensure that each part of the triplet is even and the numbers 1 2 3 4 land exactly on the beat. Most digital metronomes can be adjusted to play triplets. Adjust the setting and listen to the metronome first if you are unsure whether you have understood this rhythm.

In the following exercises, you will play eighth note triplets on the snare and toms. Start with your right hand and keep alternating throughout. You will notice that your right hand will play beats 1 and 3 while the left hand plays beats 2 and 4. Practise at a slow tempo and ensure that both hands are accurate and even. As always try to reverse the sticking in order to strengthen your hands equally.

1

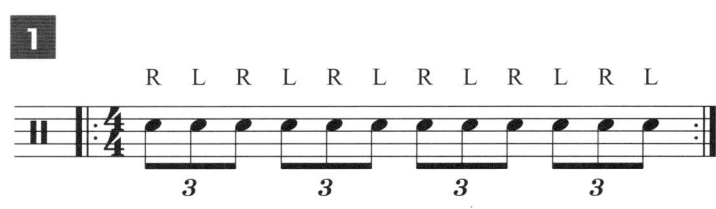

3

2

4

The Eighth Note Triplet Rest

Now let's add some rests to the triplet patterns. Continue to count the triplet rhythm and use the sticking combination that feels most natural for your technique.

The exercises are written on the snare drum, but once you have mastered them feel free to move them around the kit to create your own phrases.

5

7

6

8

Triplets With Accents

Adding accents to any pattern makes it more interesting and gives it shape. Practise the following exercises with alternating sticking and focus on keeping the unaccented strokes even and much softer than the accented strokes. Aim to achieve fluent movement of the hands and consistent triplet feel. When you feel ready try reversing the sticking.

1
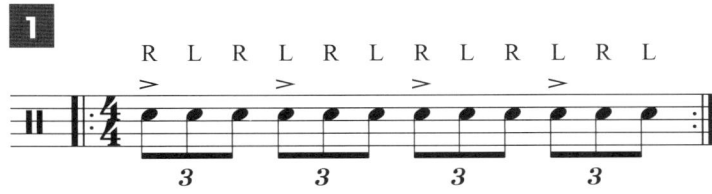

3
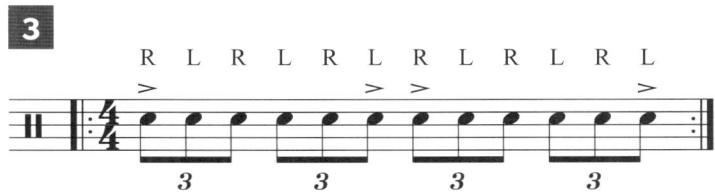

2
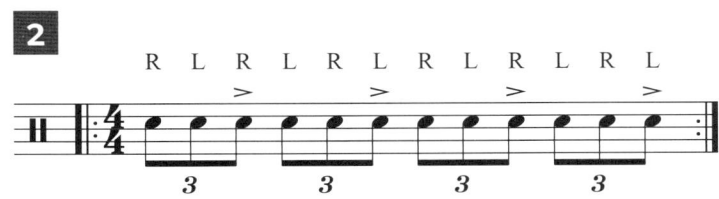

4
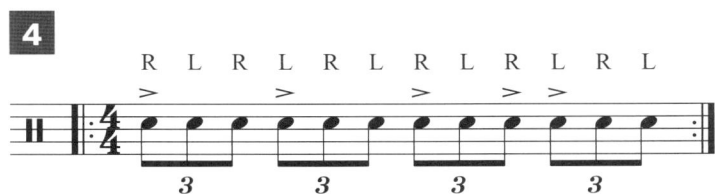

Triplets With Alternate Sticking Patterns

Playing triplets with alternating sticking will significantly improve your technique and balance between hands. However, it is also very important to practise triplets with other sticking patterns. Let's use the exercises with accents from the top of the page with different sticking patterns. Practise the exercises on the snare initially and when you feel ready start moving them around the kit using the toms and cymbals.

5
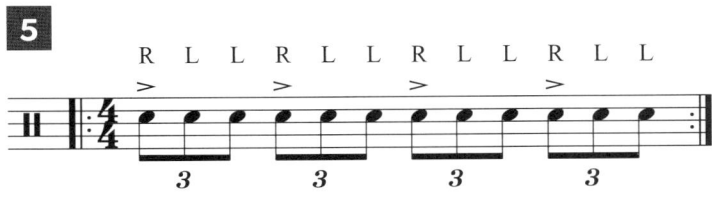

7
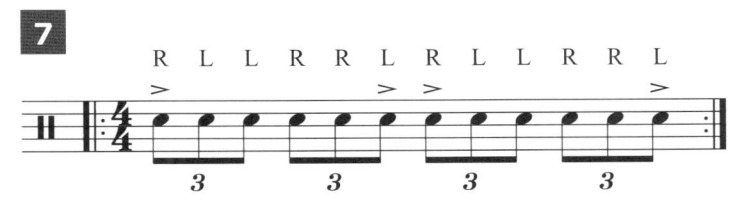

6

8

Rudiments and Technique

Flam

This drum rudiment consists of two notes which are played very close together (one with each hand). The first stroke is a tap stroke which is soft and the second will be a full stroke (much louder). Play the full stroke on the beat and the tap stroke just before. Remember that when playing a tap stroke, the drumstick should be positioned close to the drumhead. However, when

playing a full stroke the drumstick should be lifted in preparation as this will help you produce louder sound naturally. If necessary refer back to p. 13 of this book, where these drum strokes are explained.

Practise Exercise 1 at various tempos and aim to produce balanced sound from both hands.

1

Drag

The drag is very similar in concept to the flam – the only difference is that you have to play two tap strokes before the main full stroke. The soft tap strokes are played with one of the hands and the following full stroke with the other hand. Aim to play even tap strokes just before the main stroke with distinctive

dynamic difference between the two types of stroke. Most importantly, do not forget that the main stroke always lands on the beat and the tap strokes should be played before it.

2

Tip!

Playing two consecutive fast strokes with one hand is an important skill in drumming which utilises the natural bounce of the stick. You will learn how to develop and use this technique further into the series. However, the more time you spend practising the drag rudiment at slow tempos the easier future techniques will be to achieve.

Ruff

This rudiment is similar in concept to the flam and drag, but here you have to play three tap strokes before the main stroke. The example below is notated with the most common ruff sticking pattern.

However, it is recommended that you try this rudiment with various sticking options in order to improve your overall coordination and control of the drum stick.

1

Practising rudiments with feet patterns will significantly improve your coordination and control of the instrument.

Try varying the feet pattern as well as adding feet patterns to the drag and flam rudiments that you studied on p. 50.

2

Multiple Bounce Roll

Also known as a *buzz roll* or *press roll* in the drumming world, this rudiment will be useful in many styles of music, but most importantly it will help you improve your stick control. It is generally notated with a 'Z' as the sound resembles a buzzing sound. In some cases the same technique is notated with three lines above the note instead of a 'Z'.

Start by striking the snare drum with your right hand and allow the stick to bounce on the drumhead as many times as possible, then follow the same process with your left hand and keep alternating hands. It is recommended that you practise this stage slow until

the motion feels secure and natural. The key is holding the stick tightly enough so it does not move left or right but loosely enough for it be able to bounce up and down.

The next stage is bringing up the tempo until the bounces of one hand start mixing with the bounces of the other hand. This will be the beginning of the multiple bounce roll sound that you want to achieve. This technique will require weeks of practice, but if you practise for a few minutes every day and persevere you will definitely get there.

3 *(Alternative Notation)*

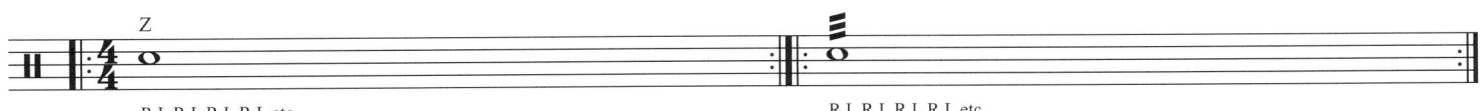

Sight Reading: Snare Drum

Quarter, Eighth, Triplet, Sixteenth and Rests

In the following exercises you will learn how to add eighth note triplets to the rhythms that you already know. Practise these at various tempos, plan your sticking and aim to achieve even strokes and consistent pulse. If you want to push yourself, try adding quarter note bass drums and different feet patterns to the exercises in order to improve your coordination.

The time signature in Exercise 5 is $\frac{3}{4}$ – this means that there are only three quarter note beats in every bar. In Exercise 6 the time signature is $\frac{6}{8}$ – this means that there are six eighth note beats in each bar. Remember to adjust your counting according to the time signature and if you are practising with a metronome, set the time signature to suit each exercise.

Unlocking the Secrets of Playing **Drums Level 1**

Sight Reading: Drum Kit

Now let's practise sight reading exercises using the whole drum kit. You will notice that the first four exercises are in $\frac{4}{4}$ while exercises 4 and 5 are in different time signatures.

Although $\frac{4}{4}$ is much more common in rock and pop, it is important that you get used to reading and playing phrases in different time signatures.

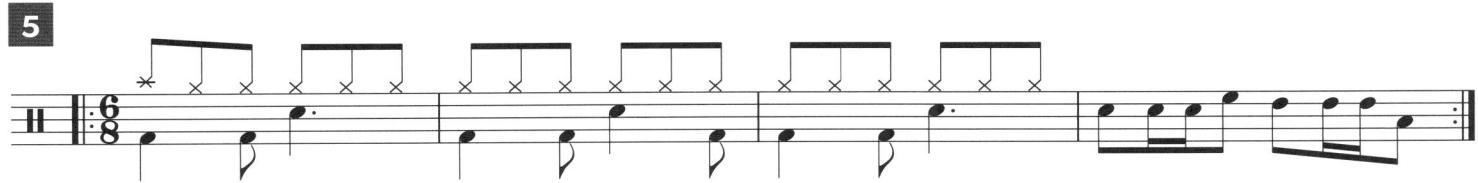

1

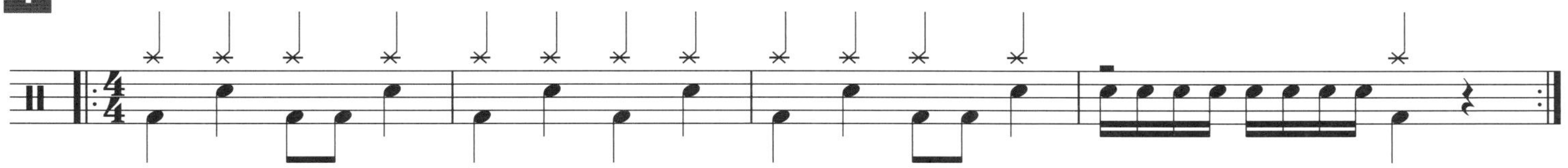

2

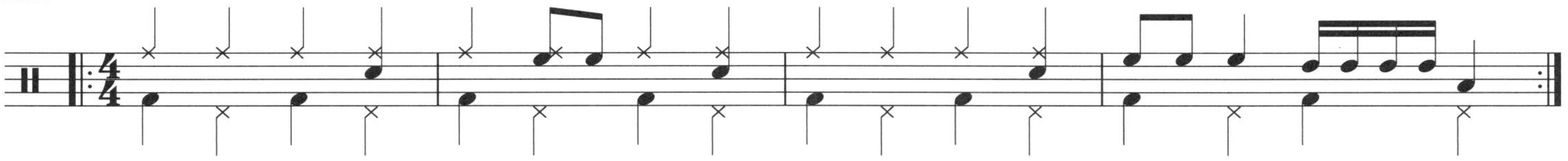

3

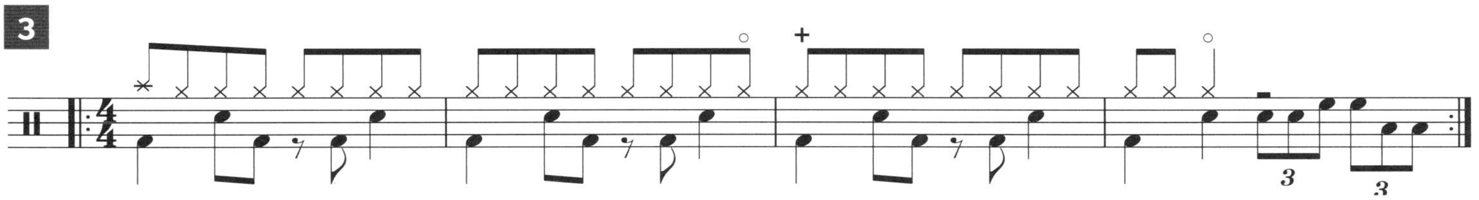

4

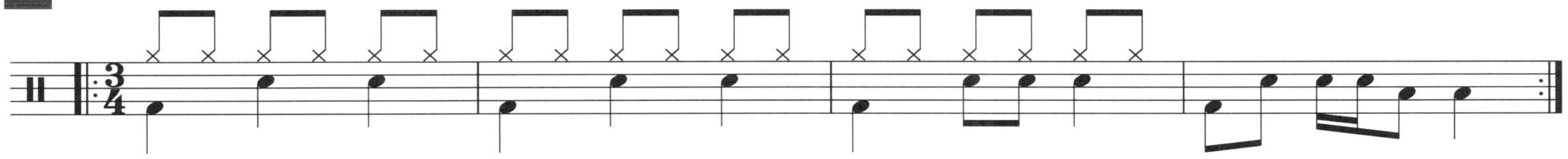

Tip!

Bars 1 and 3 of Exercise 5 contain dotted quarter notes. A dot next to a note means that the note will be longer. The exact length will be the full rhythmic value of the note plus half of its value. This means that a dotted quarter note equals one and a half quarter notes or three eighth notes.

5

Grooves

In this section you will learn some cool new grooves.

These will be divided into four groups: Rock, Funk, Blues and Latin. Therefore, when you feel comfortable with playing the grooves, you should be able to choose music that you like from each style and play along to it. This will make practice much more fun.

Remember that as the grooves are pretty basic at this stage, many of them will fit any of the styles and even work for other styles that are not yet mentioned in this book.

Rock

Funk

6/8 Blues

The blues grooves below are in the ⁶⁄₈ time signature. This means that there are six eighth notes in each bar. Counting the eighth notes (1 2 3 4 5 6) will help you to play them consistently. The snare drum should be played as cross stick. If necessary refer to p. 47 where this technique is explained in detail.

Latin

Latin grooves are known to be challenging as they require highly reliable coordination. The exercises below are examples of basic Latin grooves.

These can be easily developed to much more complex grooves at a later stage.

Drum Fills and Improvisation

Let's look at some more complex drum fills that use the rhythms and techniques that you have already learned. If necessary always feel free to refer back to the page that discussed each technique or rhythm. Practise these drum fills at various tempos and aim to achieve fluency around the kit.

The sticking pattern is up to you – spend some time, experiment with various options and find the best sticking combination according to your technique and setup. Once you have decided which sticking to use, write it in so you remember it in the future.

Grooves With Drum Fills

Now let's look at using drum fills in a musical context. The examples below are four bars long. The grooves used in the first bar are taken from pages 54 and 55.

The groove is repeated in the second and third bars, so focus on consistency of pulse here. The fourth bar consists of a one-bar drum fill that utilises ideas learned in this grade.

In the exercises below you have the opportunity to improvise and invent your own drum fills. Play the groove as written in the first bar, repeat it two more times and then play your improvised fill.

Practise this many times and find the fills that sound best to you. Aim to incorporate the rhythms and techniques that you have already learned.

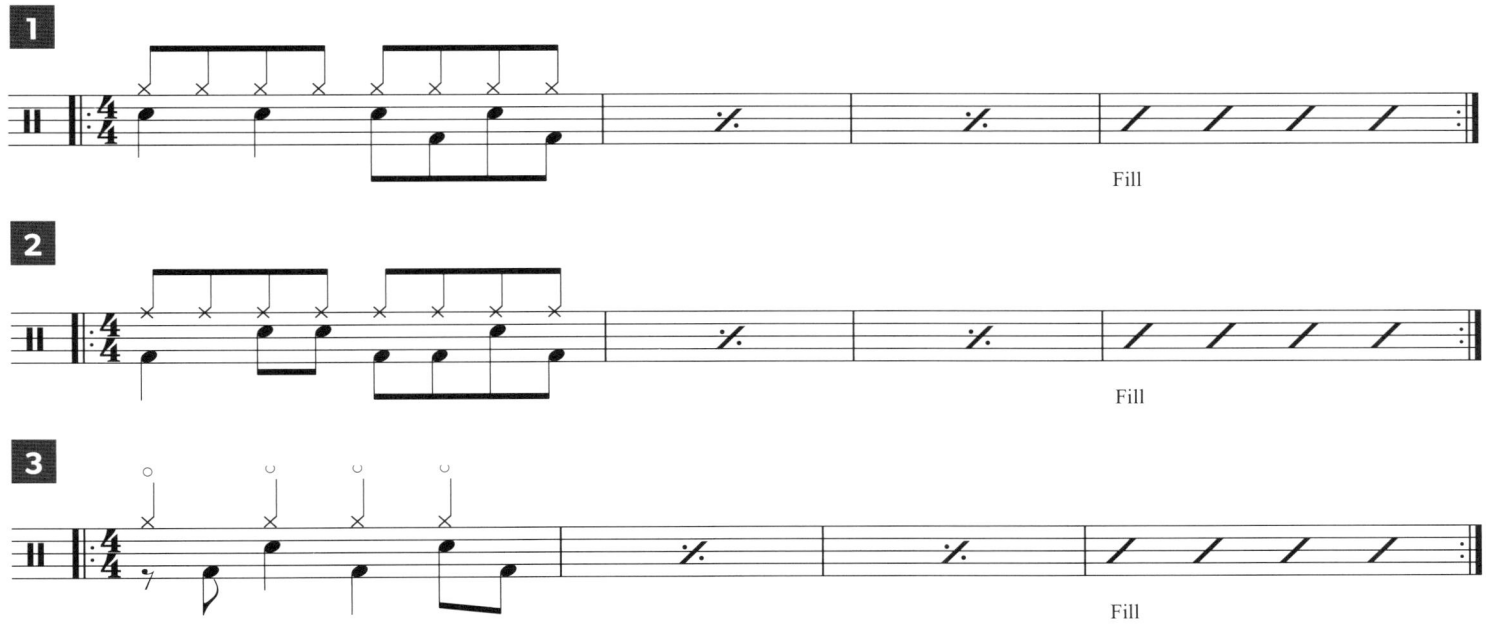

Adding Groove Variations

In the following examples you will have the opportunity to improvise around the groove. Play the groove as written in the first bar and then when you see the slashed lines feel free to add any variations that you want to the groove. When you see the word 'fill' this is the time to play your improvised fill.

You will notice that the fills in this sections vary in length. Playing fills of different lengths will make your drumming more interesting and musical. Groove variations can also be shown as 'develop', 'ad lib' and 'cont. sim' (continue in the same way). Remember that groove variations should be consistent with the character of the original groove.

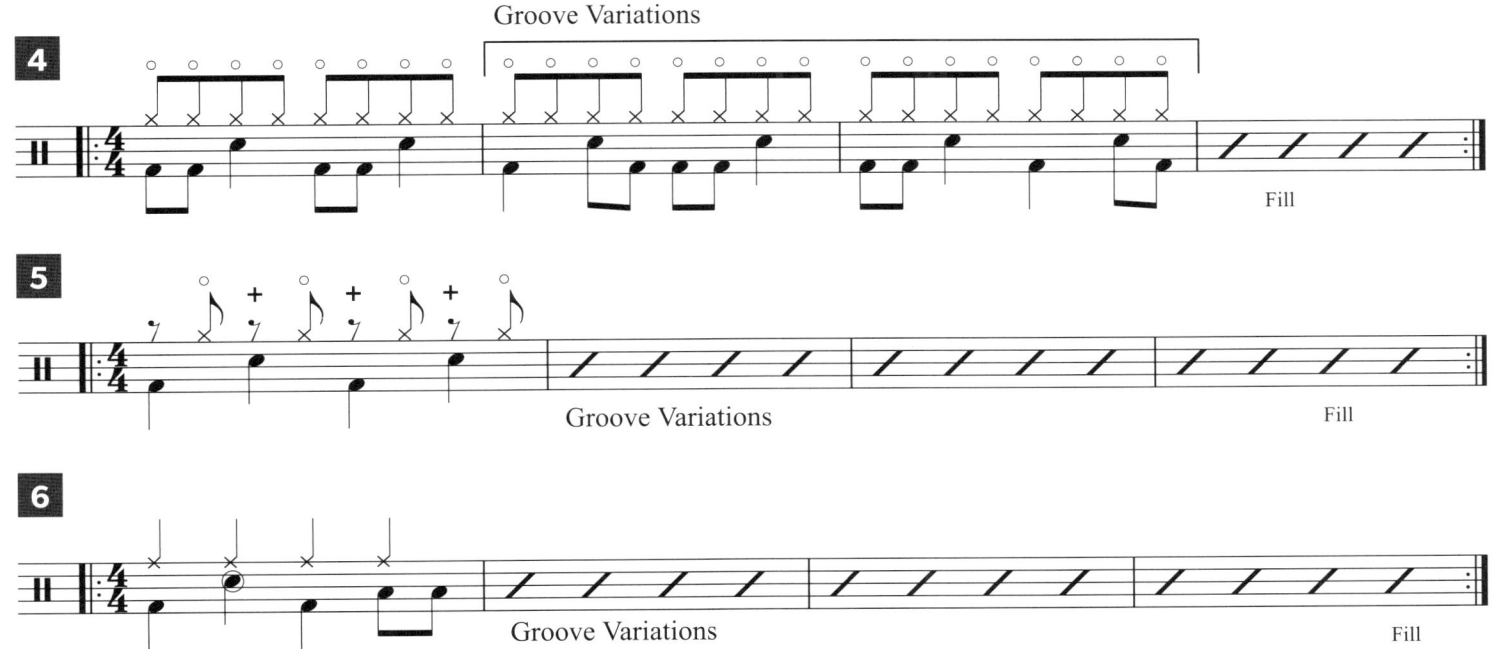

Ear Training ⏵⤸

Play each audio track without looking at the examples below.

After a count-in of four clicks, the two-bar backing is played four times. For the first and third times, listen to the recorded drums. For the second and fourth times, try to play back what you heard.

Finally, refer to the notation below to check whether you recognised the time signature, played back the exercise accurately and understand how it is written.

Rhythms

Follow the same practice method with the following three examples but note that the phrases are to be played on the snare and toms. Count the beats throughout in order to determine the time signature.

Grooves

You will notice that Exercises 1–3 are groove based. This means that more parts of the drum kit will be used. This requires secure aural understanding as you will need to recognise not only the rhythms but also the drum voices that are being played.

As explained previously, the backing track will play four times and you should attempt to play back during the second and fourth plays. The time signature on this page remains $\frac{4}{4}$, but feel free to create your own exercises in other time signatures too.

In the last three exercises of this section, there are grooves and fills. Focus on the drum voices that are being used, the rhythms and the time signature.

Practising aural skills can be a lot of fun. Follow the same method and invent some of your own exercises to help you develop further.

Getting used to playing patterns consistently for 4 bars is a great skill for drummers. When you feel comfortable with that, try practising for longer periods

of time using multiples of 4 bars such as 8, 12, 16 and even 32. Developing this skill will help you become a solid band member.

Inspirational Drummers

Ginger Baker

Ginger Baker has been described as the most influential percussionist of the 1960s. During his career with power trio Cream and the band Blind Faith he produced heavy rock beats that inspired generations of drummers of all styles. Although Baker is best known as a rock drummer, he always prefers to be known as a jazz player.

Baker became known for using two bass drums in his setup and at least four toms. With these he was able to create heavy rock beats as well as grooves with a tribal feel. Baker has always been passionate about world music, in particular African music. In 1966 Baker recorded 'Toad', a five-minute drum solo, as part of Cream's debut album. This solo has been learned and analysed by drummers all over the world for decades.

During his career, Baker was also known for using a variety of other percussion instruments and the use of African rhythms. Many of these rhythms were developed and learned during 1970–1976 when he was living in Nigeria and working closely with Afro Beat legend Fela Kuti.

Recommended Listening

'Sunshine of Your Love'
'Badge'
'White Room'

Tré Cool

Tré Cool has been the drummer of American band Green Day since 1990. He also plays in The Lookouts, Samiam and Green Day side-projects The Network and the Foxboro Hot Tubs. His fast punk drumming, together with his love of Reggae beats created his unique sound.

Cool was recruited as Green Day's drummer when only 18 years old and since then has recorded and toured with the band consistently. He has used various drums throughout his career but currently uses Gretsch drums and Zildjian cymbals. His five-piece drum kit includes bass drum, snare, high tom and two floor toms. Cool prefers large crash and ride cymbals for maximum projection from the kit.

In 2011 Cool won Best Punk Drummer in DRUM! Magazine. His drum intro for the song 'Basket Case' is regarded as one of the best drum fills ever recorded. In December 2012 Green Day released the third in a trilogy of albums entitled Tré! in his honour.

Recommended Listening

'Boulevard of Broken Dreams'
'21 Guns'
'Basket Case'

Ringo Starr

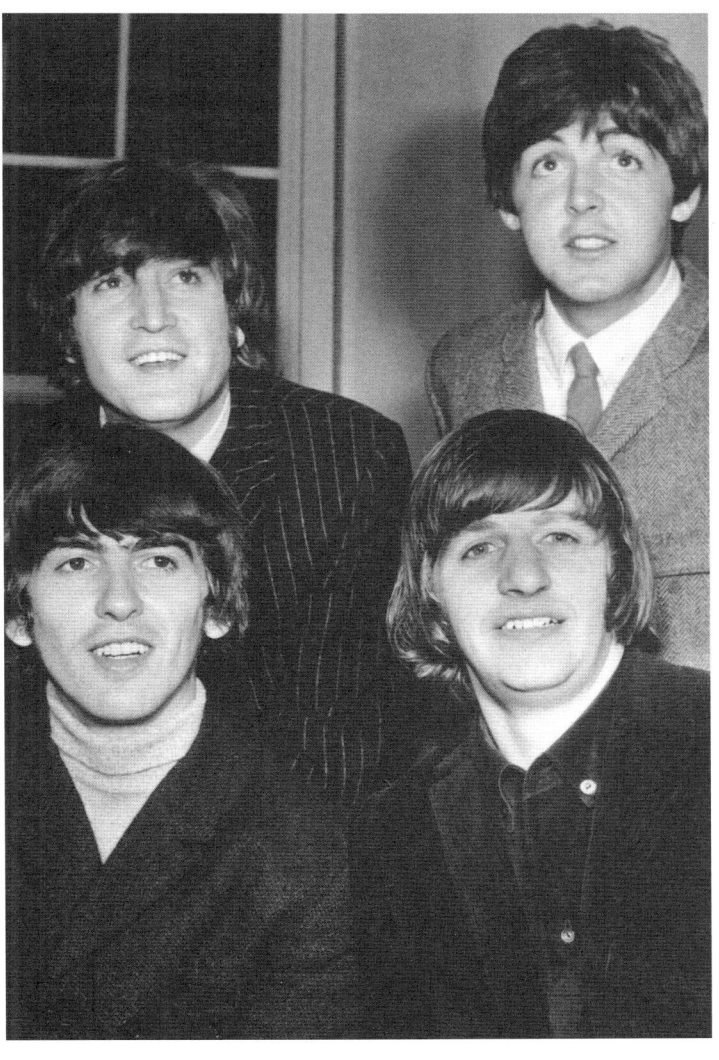

Ringo Starr was the drummer in The Beatles. He joined the band in 1962 and played a key role in their overall sound, image, films and TV appearances until their breakup in 1970. The Beatles (also known as the Fab Four) became famous worldwide in the mid 1960s and produced their finest material including some innovative and widely influential albums between 1965 and 1970. The Beatles are the best selling band in history and have inspired generations of musicians to follow their dreams and start a rock band.

The Beatles. Clockwise from top left: John Lennon, Paul McCartney, Ringo Starr, George Harrison.

Like the other members of the Beatles, Ringo pursued a solo career in the 1970s and although he initially achieved commercial and critical success with his 1973 album *Ringo*, his solo career had diminished in importance by 1975. Ringo continued to create music and in 1989 successfully toured with the twelve variations of Ringo Starr & His All-Starr Band. He was also the narrator of the first two seasons of the children's television series *Thomas The Tank Engine* and *Friends*. Ringo was honoured with a star on the Hollywood Walk of Fame in 2010.

Recommended Listening

'Come Together'
'She Loves You'
'Taxman'

'Real Deal'

The performance piece below is at Grade 2 standard. You will notice that this is significantly longer than Grade 1 and includes many of the techniques, grooves, rhythms and fills that you have learned so far.

Start by practising with a metronome and build up speed until you can play with the backing track of 'Real Deal' which can be downloaded for free from **www.vvinner.com/downloads**.

Rhythms: Swung Eighth Notes

The swung eighth note rhythm means that the eighth notes, which are usually played straight and even will be played slightly differently. Essentially, the strokes that play on the beat (1 2 3 4) remain exactly the same, so the only difference is the location of the off-beats (which are usually counted as '&'). In a swung rhythm the off-beats are played slightly later, which will actually place them closer to the next beat. Play consistent swung eighth notes on the snare and see if you can achieve this swung, jumpy feel with ease using alternate sticking. Swung rhythms can also be explained and notated with triplets.

By playing consecutive triplet eighth notes and missing the second stroke of each triplet you will be able to create exactly the same rhythm. This might look more challenging on the page, but as long as you understand the rhythm you will never have issues with reading it whichever notation method is used.

In the previous exercises you played continuous swung eighth notes in order to internalise the flow of this new rhythm. In the following exercises you will notice that there are also rests to consider. Continue to count, use the metronome if necessary and choose the sticking

combination that feels most natural for your technique. Although these exercises are written on the snare drum, once you have mastered them feel free to move them around the kit and create your own swung eighth note phrases.

Rhythms: Sixteenth Note Phrases

On this page you will learn some more complex sixteenth note phrases that can be used in various musical applications. It is important to practise the phrases slowly until you understand the rhythm.

Practising slowly will also enable your body and hands to memorise the movement and develop natural flow around the drum kit. As part of the counting below, we have notated in brackets the rhythms that should be counted but not played.

1

3

2

4

As you learned in Grade 2, adding accents to a rhythmic phrase adds shape and depth. Exercise 1 above will be used in the next four exercises to demonstrate what can be done when moving the accents around. After you have mastered **Ex. 5–8** try to do the same with **Ex. 2–4** or any other sixteenth note phrases that you like.

Moving these phrases around the kit will help you achieve creative and complex drum fills. Practise the accented phrases with various sticking combinations as this will develop your hands technique and balance between hands further.

Finally, combine the exercises in order to achieve more creative phrases.

5

7

6

8

Rudiments and Technique

Paradiddle With Accents

This fundamental drum rudiment is known to be one of the most versatile and useful tools drummers use when playing grooves, fills and even solos. In this first exercise you will notice that there are accents on the beats. When playing this exercise aim to produce a convincing full stroke on the beats and

tap strokes (much softer: keep your hands close to the drumhead) on all the unaccented strokes. When you feel comfortable, try moving the accented strokes around the toms and cymbals while maintaining the tap strokes on the snare. This will strengthen your technical control on the instrument.

Inverting Rudiments

The concept of inverting rudiments is very important in drumming. It essentially teaches you to make minor rhythmic placement changes to the rudiment in order to create a variety of musical possibilities. Although the inverted paradiddle is not one of the primary drum rudiments, it is very useful and has been used by many drummers in various styles over the years. You will notice in **Ex. 2** that the rhythm and accents remain the same. The only change is the placement of the paradiddle and therefore the sticking used on each beat.

> ### Tip!
>
> *Inverting rudiments can be quite challenging at first, but don't give up. Allowing your hands to learn a new movement and sticking combination will be very useful in the future. The process of learning a new skill (or movement) by focused repetition is at times referred to as* **muscle memory** *in drumming.*

Flam Tap

The flam tap rudiment can be notated in various rhythms but most notably is used in eighth and sixteenth notes. We will focus on the eighth note version here. As the name suggested this rudiment

consists of an accented flam followed by a softer tap stroke. The alternate sticking used will significantly help you improve the balance between the right and left hands.

Now let's try to add a feet pattern to this rudiment to challenge our coordination.

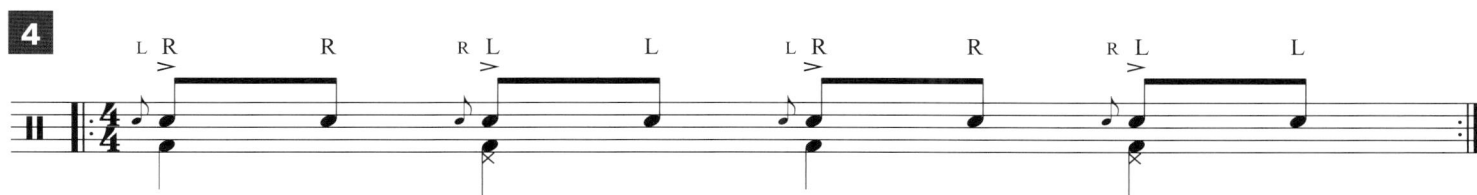

Flam Accent

In the flam accent rudiment we have consistent triplet eighth notes with accented flams on every beat. The alternating sticking can offer many musical applications on the kit.

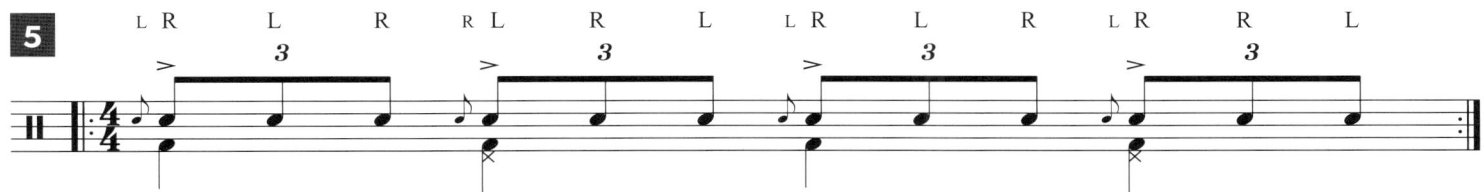

Five Stroke Roll

The five stroke roll is an integral part of drumming, regardless of the style you choose to play. It is the most basic of the stroke roll family, but if learned well the concept and technique will be easy to adjust when attempting the more complicated seven stroke roll, nine stroke roll etc.

Apart from the written notation, rhythm and accent which should be clear from the notated example below the main focus when playing this type of roll is the doubles.

You probably remember that doubles were one the first rudiments that you learned – now you have the opportunity to take this to the next level. There are various advanced techniques that will help you to produce fast and even doubles and they will be discussed in detail in higher grades. At this stage, aim to produce soft and even doubles with consistent sound from the snare drum. Differentiating between the soft doubles and accented offbeat stroke is one of the key points of this rudiment.

Sight Reading: Snare Drum

In the following exercises you will learn how to add more complex sixteenth note phrases to the rhythms that you already know. Practise these at various tempos, plan your sticking and aim to achieve even strokes and consistent pulse.

If you want to push yourself, try adding quarter note bass drums and different feet patterns to the exercises in order to improve your coordination. Remember to adjust the counting according to the time signature of each exercise.

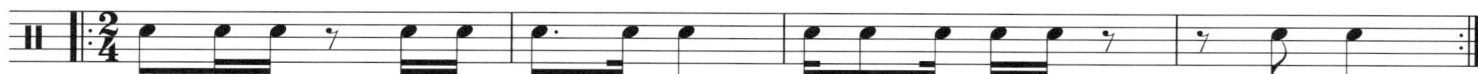

Sight Reading: Drum Kit

In this section you will learn more advanced sight reading exercises using the whole drum kit. Initially, focus on the time signature and any rhythms that seem complex. Then try to play the grooves (bars 1–3) and finally practise the fills (bar 4). When you feel confident put it all together at various tempos.

~~~
Tip!

In the fourth bar of Ex. 3 the groove breaks for a drum fill. However, the feet pattern continues consistently. Once you have developed reliable coordination it should be relatively straightforward to continue playing the feet pattern (like 'automatic pilot') while focusing on the notated drum fill.

Grooves

In this section you will learn some inspiring new grooves.

These will be divided into four groups: Rock, Funk, Shuffle and Reggae. While learning how to play these grooves it is recommended that you listen to some of the famous artists that play in each style.

You can also try to play the grooves with your favourite music from each style. The Recommended Listening section on p. 80 will be a good starting point.

Rock

Funk

At this level, the basic rock and funk beats can be similar. Therefore, many rock grooves can be used in funk music and vice versa. However, in contrast to the heavy rock grooves notated above, the following

funk grooves have more of a syncopated and light feel. Syncopation in drumming generally means that there are accents or important strokes in unexpected places in the bar.

Shuffle

In this section you will learn how to use the swung eighth notes you learned earlier in this grade in order to create the shuffle groove.

Remember that the consistent swung eighth notes on the hi-hat can be your anchor while you focus on the variations in the bass drum and snare patterns.

Reggae

This reggae groove might be challenging at first, mainly because there is no bass drum on the first beat of the bar. It can also be slightly off-putting that the main weight of the groove is not on the second and fourth beats in the bar (as in most rock and pop

grooves) but on the third beat. Aim to produce a convincing and warm sound from the cross stick and play all the accented hi-hats accurately. Practise these grooves with both straight and swung eighth notes.

Drum Fills and Improvisation

Drum Fills

Let's look at some more complex drum fills that use the rhythms and techniques that you have learned so far. If necessary, always feel free to refer back to the page that discussed each technique or rhythm.

Practise these drum fills at various tempos and aim to achieve fluency around the kit. The sticking pattern is up to you – spend some time experimenting and finding the best option for your technique and setup.

Grooves With Drum Fills

Now let's look at how to use the drum fills you have learned in a musical context. Practise each exercise until it feels comfortable. Aim to keep the pulse consistent, play along with the metronome or any of

your favourite tracks. Then, try playing each exercise with the repeat (twice) and move to the next without stopping. This will help you move between different grooves seamlessly.

Improvisation

In the exercises below you have the opportunity to improvise and invent your own drum fills. Play the groove as written in bar 1, repeat it twice more and then play your improvised fill. Practise this many times and find the fills that sound best to you.

Aim to incorporate the rhythms and techniques that you have learned so far. Listening to drummers that play each style of music convincingly will help you understand what improvised fills and groove variations are appropriate in each style.

Groove Variations

In this section you have the opportunity to improvise around the groove as well as playing your own drum fill. The only bar that must be played as notated is the first bar, then in bars 2 and 3 you need to embellish

the groove and complete the four bar exercise with an improvised fill. It is important that you start the fill exactly on the beat where the word 'fill' appears.

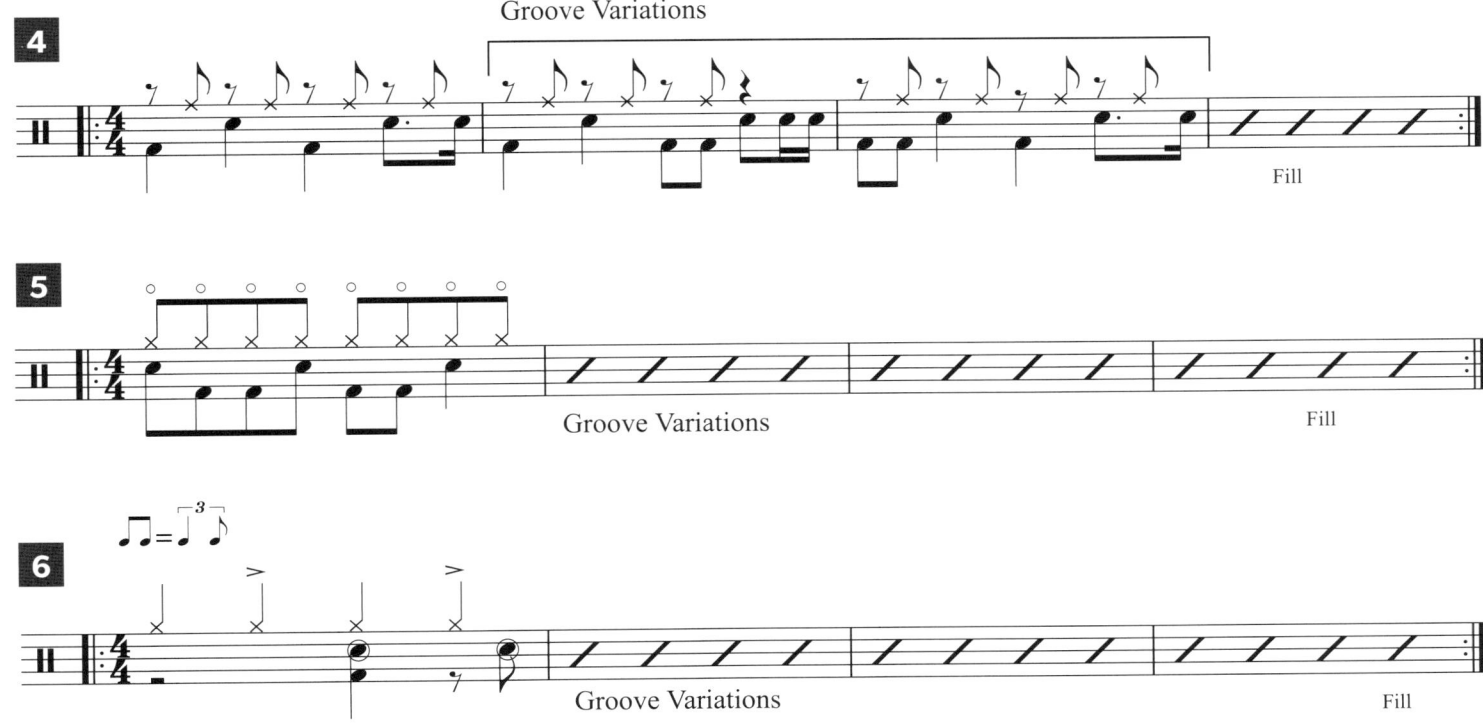

Ear Training ⏯↻

Play each audio track without looking at the examples below.

After a count-in of four clicks, the two-bar backing is played four times. For the first and third times, listen to the recorded drums. For the second and fourth times, try to play back what you heard.

Finally, refer to the notation below to check whether you recognised the time signature, played back the exercise accurately and understand how it is written.

Rhythms

Follow the same practice method with the following three examples but note that the phrases are to be played on the snare and toms.

There are no accents in these exercises. Count the beats throughout in order to determine the time signature.

Grooves

You will notice that Exercises 1–3 are groove based. This means that more parts of the drum kit will be used. This requires secure aural understanding as you will not only have to recognise the rhythms but also the drum voices that are being played.

As explained previously, the backing track will play four times and you should attempt to play back during the second and fourth plays. The time signature on this page remains $\frac{4}{4}$, but feel free to create your own exercises in other time signatures too.

In the last three exercises of this section, there are grooves and fills. Focus on the drum voices that are being used, the rhythms and the time signature.

Practising aural skills can be a lot of fun. Follow the same method and invent some of your own exercises to help you develop further.

Listen to some of your favourite songs and see if you can understand, play and even write out the grooves and fills that you hear.

This process will really help you improve your aural skills and most importantly develop your own sound on the drums.

Inspirational Drummers

Dave Grohl

Dave Grohl became widely famous in 1990 as the drummer of grunge band Nirvana. From 1990 to 1994 Grohl recorded and toured extensively with Nirvana until the sudden death of frontman Kurt Cobain in April 1994. The band's albums *Nevermind* (1991) and *In Utero* (1993) were massively successful and many of the tracks on these albums became classics. Apart from drums, Grohl contributed to the songwriting and provided distinctive backing vocals. He also constantly developed his own material, playing all instruments and singing.

In late 1994 Grohl starting formalising his own ideas with some of his favourite musicians; this project has become his main focus and the band is now known as the Foo Fighters. The band has continuously grown in popularity worldwide and has become known for its propulsive live performances. The multi-talented Grohl decided to be the guitarist and main vocalist, leaving the drum throne to his good friend Taylor Hawkins. Outside of Foo Fighters, Grohl has played drums for rock supergroup Them Crooked Vultures, Queens Of The Stone Age and artists including Tom Petty, David Bowie, Iggy Pop and Paul McCartney.

Recommended Listening

'Smells Like Teen Spirit'
'In Bloom'
'Lithium'

Travis Barker

Rolling Stone magazine referred to **Travis Barker** as Punk's first superstar drummer. Barker is best known as the drummer in Blink 182. However, he also performed with the bands +44, The Transplants and Box Car Racer and worked with artists such as Game, Tom Morello, RZA, Slash, Raekwon and Corey Taylor. Barker released his debut solo album *Give the Drummer Some* in 2011.

In 1999 Barker founded the clothing company Famous Stars and Straps which became very successful. Nowadays, Barker is not only a drum icon but also a fashion guru that consistently develops products and collaborates with companies such as DC Shoes, Orange County Drum and Percussion and Zildjian.

Barker has made over a dozen appearances on TV shows and movies throughout his career as well as being a playable character on video games *Guitar Hero* and *Tony Hawk*.

Recommended Listening

'All the Small Things'
'What's My Age Again?'
'When I Was Young'

John Bonham

Led Zeppelin. From left to right: John Paul Jones, John Bonham, Jimmy Page, Robert Plant.

John Bonham is best known as the drummer for Led Zeppelin. He is famous for his speed, power, fast right foot, distinctive sound and unique feel. Bonham is widely considered to be one of the greatest drummers in the history of rock music. Bonham was Led Zeppelin's drummer from 1968 until his premature and sudden death in 1980. His feel and drive were an integral part of the band's overall sound. Bonham was known for using very big drums by the drum company Ludwig and the 2002 series from the cymbal manufacturer Paiste. His live setup also included timpani, cowbells and a gong.

Bonham's famous drum solo on the track 'Moby Dick' became one of the iconic drum solos in rock history. The solo has been analysed by many musical experts and has inspired generations of drummers up to the present day. In Led Zeppelin's live performances the drum solo of 'Moby Dick' would often last for 30 minutes and regularly featured Bonham's use of bare hands on the drums.

Recommended Listening

'Immigrant Song'
'When the Levee Breaks'
'Kashmir'

'Groove On' ⏯

The performance piece below is at Grade 3 standard.

Notice that the techniques, grooves, rhythms and fills that are slightly harder than Grade 2 standard. Studying this piece carefully will ensure that you have understood many of the subjects that were taught in this grade before moving to the next grade.

Take your time and practise each section separately before putting it together. Practising with a metronome and the backing track provided will make the practice more fun and help you maintain a steady pulse. The 'Groove On' backing track and full demo can be downloaded for free from **www.vvinner.com/ downloads**.

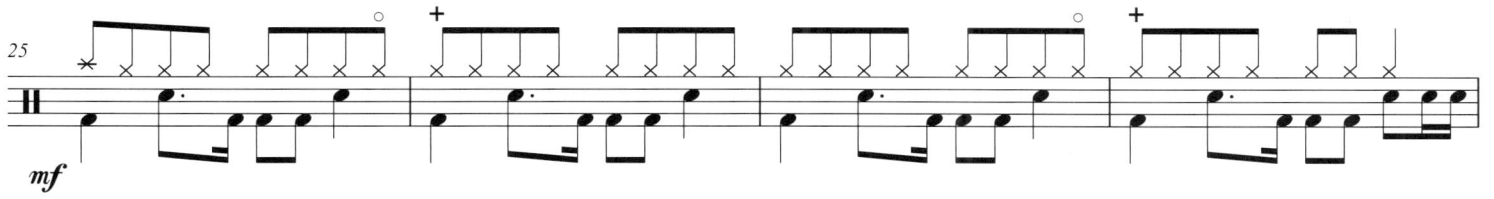

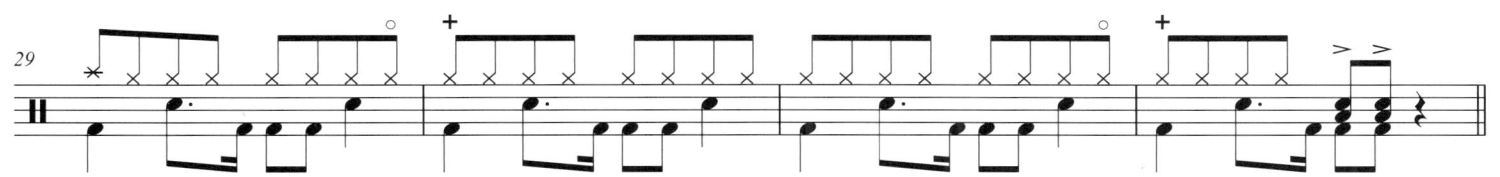

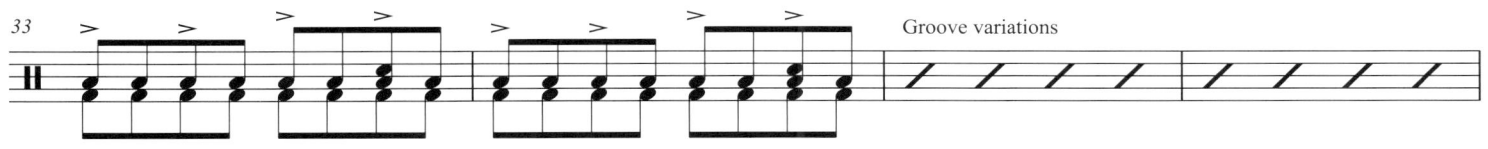

Groove variations

Fill

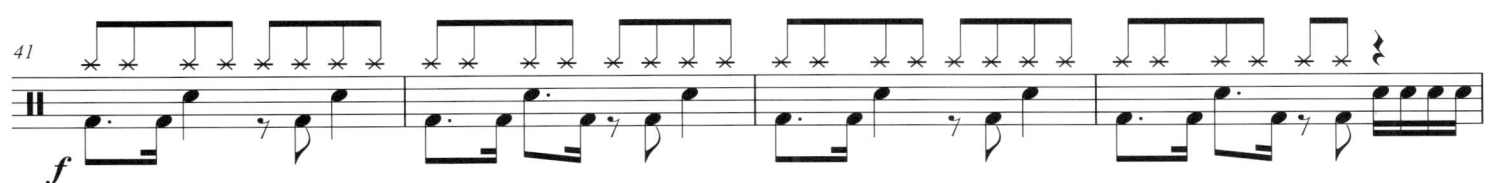

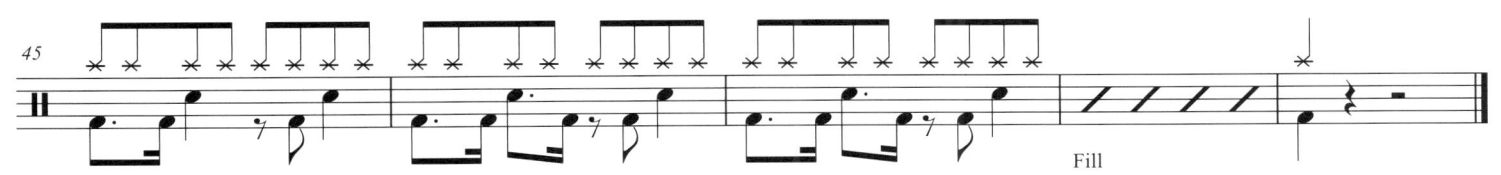

Fill

About the Author

Noam Lederman is a musician, educator and author based in the UK. He has built a successful music career combining performance and writing. He has written more than 100 music publications that have sold over a million copies worldwide.

Noam has a postgraduate degree in Jazz from the Guildhall School of Music and Drama. He has worked with renowned musicians such as Billy Cobham, Dave Liebman, Kenny Wheeler, Corinne Bailey Rae, State of Bengal, Mark Hill and Trevor Horn.

Noam has performed at many music festivals including Womad, Glastonbury, Reading and Sonar as well as appearing on MTV. He regularly performs at various events across the globe, thus continuing to develop his instrumental skills.

After being a music examiner for many years, in 2009 Noam was appointed Chief Examiner for the international music board Rockschool. In 2014 Noam founded the company VVinner Music which provides high quality educational products and services to music institutions.

In April 2015 Noam was appointed as the Principal of The Academy of Rock - an award winning franchise of music schools in Asia.

Noam continues to inspire and educate as an academic consultant working with music institutions, schools and teachers worldwide to raise their standards and be the best in their field.

For more information or if you wish to contact the author please visit **www.noamlederman.com**.

Recommended Listening

One of the most important things any aspiring musician should do is to listen. All the great music you will ever hear has been built on foundations supplied by earlier musicians. Listen to as much as you can, in as many different styles. The list here represents just a few starting points in some important styles, in addition to the drummers mentioned earlier in this book.

Rock/Pop

Neil Peart
Ian Paice
Mitch Mitchell
Vinnie Colaiuta
Steve Smith
Aaron Spears
John J.R. Robinson
Terry Bozzio

Heavy Rock/Metal

Danny Carey
Lars Ulrich
Dave Lombardo
Mike Portnoy
Joey Jordison
Bill Ward

Funk/Blues

Clyde Stubblefield
Jabo Starks
Zigaboo 'Ziggy' Modeliste
David Garibaldi
Chad Smith
Steve Gadd
Steve Jordan
Jeff Porcaro
Bernard Purdie

Jazz/World

Buddy Rich
Elvin Jones
Tony Williams
Bill Bruford
Carlton 'Carly' Barrett
Tony Allen
Horacio 'El Negro' Hernandez
Alex Acuña